T0328764

Cambridge Elements ≡

Cambridge Elements in International Economics
edited by
Kenneth A. Reinert
George Mason University

EXPORT QUALITY AND INCOME DISTRIBUTION

Rajat Acharyya
Jadavpur University

Shrimoyee Ganguly
Jadavpur University

CAMBRIDGE
UNIVERSITY PRESS

Shaftesbury Road, Cambridge CB2 8EA, United Kingdom

One Liberty Plaza, 20th Floor, New York, NY 10006, USA

477 Williamstown Road, Port Melbourne, VIC 3207, Australia

314–321, 3rd Floor, Plot 3, Splendor Forum, Jasola District Centre,
New Delhi – 110025, India

103 Penang Road, #05–06/07, Visioncrest Commercial, Singapore 238467

Cambridge University Press is part of Cambridge University Press & Assessment,
a department of the University of Cambridge.

We share the University's mission to contribute to society through the pursuit of
education, learning and research at the highest international levels of excellence.

www.cambridge.org
Information on this title: www.cambridge.org/9781009124607

DOI: 10.1017/9781009128995

© Rajat Acharyya and Shrimoyee Ganguly 2023

This publication is in copyright. Subject to statutory exceptionand to the provisions
of relevant collective licensing agreements, no reproduction of any part may take
place without the written permission of Cambridge University Press & Assessment.

First published 2023

A catalogue record for this publication is available from the British Library.

ISBN 978-1-009-12460-7 Paperback
ISSN 2753-9326 (online)
ISSN 2753-9318 (print)

Cambridge University Press & Assessment has no responsibility for the persistence
or accuracy of URLs for external or third-party internet websites referred to in this
publication and does not guarantee that any content on such websites is, or will remain,
accurate or appropriate.

Export Quality and Income Distribution

Cambridge Elements in International Economics

DOI: 10.1017/9781009128995

First published online: January 2023

Rajat Acharyya
Jadavpur University

Shrimoyee Ganguly
Jadavpur University

Author for correspondence: Rajat Acharyya, rajat.acharyya@gmail.com

Abstract: Given the increasing sensitivity of buyers in richer countries towards the quality of the goods that they consume, low-quality exports largely constrain the export growth of developing countries. This Element documents attempts to estimate cross-country quality variations and reviews the demand-side and supply-side explanations for the low-export-quality phenomenon. It examines how trade policies can incentivise export quality upgrading and discusses the underlying channels through which a reverse causality – export quality causing within-country income or wage inequality to worsen – may develop. This issue of wage inequality assumes relevance because export-promotion policies may be difficult to sustain in such situations, particularly in large democracies where political risks from inequality-driven conflict are quite high.

Keywords: Export quality, income distribution, low-export-quality phenomenon, trade policies, labour market implications

© Rajat Acharyya and Shrimoyee Ganguly 2023

ISBNs: 9781009124607 (PB), 9781009128995 (OC)
ISSNs: 2753-9326 (online), 2753-9318 (print)

Contents

1 Introduction

New evidence emerging over the last two decades reveals the importance of non-price dimensions in the export performances of developing countries and in export-led growth. The most important of such non-price dimensions is quality of exports, which has emerged as one of the key competitive variables of marketing strategy. For example, using Chinese firm-level export prices, Manova and Zhang (2012) find some evidence of quality sorting in exports. Dongwen et al. (2016), in their study on China's agri-food export, find that the exporters with higher product quality capture more demand and opportunities in the world market. The findings of AbdGhani, NikMat and Sulaiman (2019) reveal that the role of product quality is important in influencing the export performance of Malaysian electric and electronic goods. Similarly, the survey of export manufacturers in New Zealand by Thirkell and Dau (1998) finds that product quality significantly affects their export performance. Fischer (2010) estimates that European Union (EU) agribusiness competitiveness can be enhanced by exporting better-quality products to the increasingly liberalised and quality-conscious markets. Evidence from India's manufacturing sector in 1989–97 also supports the notion that *quality matters in the export market under perceived quality uncertainty* (Das and Bandyopadhyay, 2003). On the other hand, Verhoogen (2008) argues that higher-productivity firms in comparison to low-productivity firms in the same industries would gain more export opportunities by improving product quality.

Evidence from cross-country studies on export-led growth also suggests that what matters is not *how much* a country exports but *what* it exports. Growth rates are observed to be much higher for countries that export high-quality, high-technology-intensive and sophisticated products than countries exporting low-quality products (Hausmann and Klinger, 2006; Rodrik, 2006; Hausmann, Hwang and Rodrik, 2007; Bayudan-Dacuycuy and Lim, 2014). Similarly, simulation results by Hidalgo et al. (2007) suggest that the exports of the lagging developing countries will not be as sophisticated as the exports of industrialised economies. Didier and Pinat (2013), on the other hand, observe that higher human capital intensity of traded goods creates a positive spillover effect on economic growth.

There are both demand and supply sides to this quality dimension determining export performance and export-led growth. On the demand side, with the rise in income levels, buyers in the advanced industrialised world have become more quality-conscious and are more sensitive to quality variations than to price variations of the goods they consume. Accordingly, they prefer to buy goods of higher quality at higher prices than to compromise on lower quality for cheaper prices. An earlier postulate in this regard was the Linder (1961) hypothesis: richer countries spend a larger proportion of their income on high-quality goods, and this makes them producers of high-quality goods. More recent evidence is provided by Hallak (2006), who finds that richer countries have a relatively stronger demand for high-unit-value imports – usually considered an indirect measure of export quality – and that these higher-quality goods are imported disproportionately from the higher-income countries. Other studies suggest that wealthier households typically consume goods of higher quality (Bils and Klenow, 2001; Broda and Romalis, 2011). This sets a demand constraint for goods being exported by developing countries to advanced industrialised countries.

On the supply side, developing countries typically produce cheaper goods of lower quality. For example, the findings of many studies indicate a positive association between per capita income and quality of exports (Schott, 2004; Hummels and Klenow, 2005; Hallak and Schott, 2011). This sets a quality constraint and induces richer countries to impose minimum quality standards on goods imported from developing countries. There are a variety of reasons for the low-export-quality phenomenon in developing countries: major explanations include backward technologies and low rates of innovation; highly skewed income distribution and corresponding low domestic demand for higher-quality varieties; and asymmetric information regarding product quality and foreign buyers' poor country-of-origin perception of goods imported from low-income developing countries. In many cases, by eliminating foreign competition, restrictive trade policies in developing counties discourage the domestic firms from undertaking in-house quality-upgrading innovations.

These demand and supply constraints on export growth for developing countries, together with the quality regulations imposed by developed countries, render traditional cost-reducing and demand-generating export-promotion policies (such as export subsidies, tariff reductions and devaluation) mostly ineffective. For policies to successfully promote exports, developing countries now need to focus on the quality dimension, instead of the price dimension, of their export goods. Moreover, given the recent evidence on the importance of the availability of specific skills and of capital and consequent domestic-factor costs for the quality choices made by exporting firms (Brambilla, Lederman and Porto, 2012, 2019; Brambilla and Porto, 2016), any export-promotion policy must affect the domestic factor cost of quality favourably. Since often any policy change causes prices of capital and skill to vary in opposite directions, the specific technology underlying quality upgrading holds the key in this context. For example, if higher-quality varieties of an export good require more intensive use of skilled labour relative to capital, then a policy that lowers the skilled wage relative to the rate of return to capital will lower the marginal cost of quality and consequently incentivise quality upgrading. This suggests that a trade policy would affect the quality of export goods by changing relative factor prices and, correspondingly, redistributing factor incomes. This supply-side link between domestic income distribution and export quality is the central theme of the analysis of Acharyya and Jones (2001). At the same time, since technological requirements for upgrading the quality of different export goods may vary, a policy may have an asymmetric impact on these goods' quality levels, as has been demonstrated in Ganguly and Acharyya (2021, 2022a) of late. This lends a theoretical justification to the observed asymmetric variations in quality of goods for countries such as Brazil, China and India, during their liberalisation periods.

There is also a reverse causality between export quality and within-country income distribution. Since higher-quality varieties usually require more intensive use of skilled labour than do lower-quality varieties, quality upgrading induced by an export-promotion policy raises the demand for skilled labour and, correspondingly, the skilled labour wage. This may accentuate wage inequality between skilled and unskilled workers. Moreover, if quality upgrading and production expansion of export goods require more capital as well, production in the rest of the economy may contract due to the overall scarcity of capital. Unskilled workers employed in other sectors thus may be adversely hit. Jobs lost for them either cannot be compensated through employment elsewhere if there are already unemployed workers in the economy due to downward rigid wages, or may be compensated through low-wage jobs in the informal labour markets, a typical feature of the segmented labour markets in developing countries. In either case, the wage inequality worsens. This reverse causality has been recently formalised in Ganguly and Acharyya (2021). Consequently, export-promotion policies may be difficult to sustain, particularly in large democracies where political risks from inequality-driven conflict are quite high.

In this Element we put together this two-way causality and the development paradox in a comprehensive analytical framework. We highlight the underlying causes of the low-export-quality phenomenon, the nature of export-promotion policies to incentivise quality upgrading, and the labour market implications thereof. In Section 2 we discuss the measurement issues and document the wide variations in export quality across countries. Section 3 elaborates upon different theoretical explanations for the low-export-quality phenomenon and related empirical evidence. Trade and export-promotion policies affecting export quality through redistribution of factor incomes are discussed in Section 4. In Section 5 we analyse the reverse causation, namely, whether and how quality variations affect domestic income distribution and, more precisely, wage inequality between skilled and unskilled workers. In this context we highlight the segmented labour markets – coexistence of formal and informal labour markets – that are typical in most of the developing countries. Section 6 examines the role of domestic demand for quality-differentiated export goods; monopoly production of such goods; and implications of policies affecting the choice of export quality for the level of employment of unskilled workers when they are not fully employed. Finally, Section 7 summarises the discussions.

2 Export Quality: Measurement Issues and Cross-Country Estimates

The emerging role of export quality as one of the key determinants for export performance and consequent growth prospects has brought to the forefront the need for empirical estimates of policy effects on export quality and how those can be designed to promote quality upgrading. The biggest challenge for researchers and analysts in this regard has been measuring and quantifying product quality appropriate for cross-country comparisons. The quality of a product is often subjective, multidimensional and, most importantly, relative.[1] Each product is characterised by a number of specific features concerning its reliability, brand, design, performance, durability and safety, among others. Moreover, the level of quality of one product is usually defined in relative terms, i.e. by drawing reference to the quality levels of other, comparable products.

This section begins with a brief review of the expanding literature on these measurement issues concerning export quality. Next we present a series of stylised facts about export quality and how it varies across rich and poor nations. This helps us to reflect upon the low-export-quality phenomenon in developing countries.

2.1 Measuring Product Quality

The earliest attempts to measure quality wereby Feenstra (1994) and, subsequently, Broda and Weinstein (2006). Using constant elasticity of substitution (CES)–type utility functions, Feenstra (1994) constructed a price index allowing for different sets of product varieties and quality variations in them over time. However, in a demand and supply equilibrium, if the new varieties are not taken into account it results in a bias; the extent of the bias depends on the elasticity of substitution between all the varieties. Feenstra's (1994) solution was to estimate the elasticity of substitution between varieties from each

---

[1] There is also the problem of observability. While the quality of some goods can be discerned at the time of purchase, that of many other products, particularly durables, cannot be judged a priori.

country using the generalised method of moments.[2] In contrast, Schott (2004), Hummels and Klenow (2005), Hallak (2006) and, more recently, Fan, Li and Yeaple (2018) use as a proxy for product quality the unit value, i.e. the observable average trade price for each product category. The idea here is that higher-quality goods sell at higher prices and higher price signals higher quality. However, unit values are noisy proxies as they are driven by a series of other factors, including production cost differences such as wage differentials. Moreover, changes in unit values over time may reflect changes in quality-adjusted prices (owing to supply or demand shocks), rather than changes in quality itself. So unit-value-equivalent quality estimates fail to differentiate across the vertical (e.g., comfort) and horizontal (e.g., style) attributes that products possess. This is what Amiti and Khandelwal (2009) and Khandelwal (2010) built upon. In their measure of quality, when two products have identical unit values, the product with the higher market share is assigned higher quality, the amount depending on the slope of the demand schedule. To estimate quality, they use a nested logit demand framework based on Berry (1994), where they define quality as the vertical component of the model and assign astructural definition to it as the mean valuation that US consumers attach to an imported product. In a discrete-choice framework, higher quality identified with higher market share will act as a parallel demand shifter. However, what they missed out is that other factors such as changes in tastes will also affect export market shares. That is, there may be shifts in the demand curve *not* induced by a change in export quality. As pointed out by Vandenbussche (2014), a product of a certain quality exported by a country could have different market shares in two destination countries due to the differences in preferences among the consumers in the two markets. So, taking into account additional demand-shifting parameters gives a more unbiased measure of quality. When there is a change in the market share of two different varieties of a product in the destination country, one can thus differentiate whether it is due to a change in the quality (if there is a vertical demand shift) or to a change in tastes (if there is a slope shift).[3]

Vandenbussche (2014) also criticised the earlier CES approach of Feenstra (1994) by arguing that CES across varieties fails to distinguish between vertical and horizontal differentiation. Despite introducing a firm-product-specific

---

[2] Later, Benkovskis and Wörz (2012) pointed out a shortcoming of the CES estimation procedure, i.e. that it is likely that the substitution elasticity between the product varieties is overestimated, which further leads to excessive volatility on quality.

[3] The market share of high-quality goods such as Apple's iPhone or MacBook may also be low in developing countries because very few people there can afford to buy them. Thus, market share may not be an appropriate indicator of quality. We will return to this ability-to-pay argument as a plausible cause of inferior qualities being produced in poor countries in Section 3.

demand shock that accounts for sales variation of the same firm-product across countries without affecting prices (Bernard, Redding and Schott, 2011), this issue remains unresolved. So a well-defined set of consumer preferences is necessary to clearly differentiate quality differences from taste differences across product varieties. Di Comite, Thisse and Vandenbussche (2014) came up with a clearer approach in which they tried to disentangle the interplay of horizontal and vertical differentiation to infer which shifts in demand are actually attributable to changes in quality. They argued that changes in taste will induce variations in the quantities of the variety demanded but not affect the willingness to pay. Using an extended Melitz–Ottaviano (2008) model and Belgian firm-product data, they considered quality differences between firms as firm-specific parallel demand shocks, in addition to productivity differences, that determine firms' export market performance. They generated an indicator for unobservable quality using export prices (unit values) and product-level mark-ups created from firm-level data on variable input costs and sales. They also captured competition effects in the destination market as the consumption of all substitute products available to consumers there. However, as they could not meet the data requirements to assign a quality level to each product, the quality measure obtained by them is only a relative quality ranking of each product as compared to other competitors of the same product in Europe.

Other strategies for quality estimation looked at addressing country-specific issues for short periods of time and few product varieties. For example, Khandelwal (2010) analysed the effect of import competition on quality upgrading in the United States, mainly aiming to establish that low wage competition in the United States causes bigger losses in employment and output levels for US sectors with short quality ladders. Following Khandelwal (2010) and Hallak and Sivadasan (2013), Hu, Parsely and Tan (2017) defined quality as any attribute other than price that raises consumers' demand, to examine the effect of appreciation of domestic currency relative to that of the source country on exported product quality using Chinese Customs data between 2000 and 2006. Similarly, while examining the effects of changes in real exchange rates using Argentinean firm-level wine export values and volumes between 2002 and 2009, Chen and Juvenal (2014) took wine ratings by two global rating systems as a measure of quality. To address the potential endogeneity of quality in explaining unit values and export volumes, they further used appropriate instruments for quality based on geography and weather-related factors.

Another novel approach was taken up more recently by Piveteau and Smagghue (2019), who attempted to identify quality from the demand side at the firm-product-destination-year level. Similar to Khandelwal (2010), they used a CES demand system but identified the quality of a product as a utility shifter, which implies that it is variations in sales and not price movements that explain export quality variations over time and across firms. They presented a new instrument for obtaining the price of firms' exports; it works by interacting firm-specific importing shares with real exchange rates and then identifying firm-level quality from residual export variations, after controlling for prices. They argue that this instrument is exogenous to both the quality choices that firms make and measurement errors on prices, which constitutes an improvement relative to the existing instruments in the literature, thereby providing consistent estimates of the demand functions using trade data. However, the methodology was applied only to French firms for a short period, from 1997 to 2010; such country-specific estimation is not suitable for making cross-country comparisons, especially those incorporating developing countries.

Henn, Papageorgiou and Spatafora (2013) fill this gap with a parallel endeavour to develop new estimates of quality taken up under the World Trade Organization (WTO) Economic Research and Statistics Division, as an International Monetary Fund–Department for Internatinal Development (IMF–DFID) research collaboration. Extending the UN–National Bureau of Economic Research (NBER) dataset, they provide us with the most extensive quality indices for 200 countries for the period 1962–2014, and covering 851 products at the United Nations (UN) Standard International Trade Classificaiton (SITC) four-digit level. The trade dataset is constructed by supplementing importer-reported data with exporter-reported data where the former does not exist. The dataset contains 45.3 million observations on bilateral trade values and quantities at the SITC four-digit level. The estimation methodology derives quality from unit values, but with two important adjustments. The methodology is a modified version of Hallak (2006). As a first step, it determines the trade price (equivalently, the unit value) for any given product. Prices reflect three factors: unobservable quality, per capita exporter income and distance between exporter and importer. This accounts for selection bias. Typically, the composition of exports to more distant destinations is tilted towards higher-priced goods because of higher shipping costs. Next, a quality-augmented gravity equation is specified, separately for each product, because preferences for quality and trade costs may vary across products. The estimation equation is then obtained by substituting observables for the unobservable quality parameter in the gravity equation. It is estimated separately for each of the 851 product categories at the SITC four-digit level. Regression coefficients are used to calculate a comprehensive set of quality estimates which are then aggregated across all importers, using current trade values as weights, and then to SITC three-digit, two-digit, one-digit and country-level aggregates. Such an extensive and detailed methodology significantly contributes to bridging the large gap that the existing methodologies have left behind. It provides a set of quality estimates with country, product and time coverage that is as wide as possible, which not only makes country-specific empirical studies comparable in terms of unified quality estimates but also creates scope for examining the underlying causal factors in a cross-country study.

2.2 Cross-Country Quality Dispersions

Henn et al. (2013) identify significant cross-country heterogeneity in the growth rate of quality. Stylised facts put forth suggest that reducing barriers to entry into new sectors can allow economies to benefit from rapid quality convergence over time. Their findings that quality upgrading is particularly rapid during the early stages of development, with the process largely completed as a country reaches upper-middle-income status, is a learning lesson for developing countries. While low-income countries suffer from the poor quality of their export products, a similar low-export-quality phenomenon can be observed for many lower-middle- and upper-middle-income countries as well.

Figure 1 reflects upon this by comparing the export quality indices of manufactured goods of some sample countries from different income subgroups with those of the United States for the period 1963–2010.[4] Note that the quality levels of primary goods such as mining extractions, tea, coffee, rice, etc., are often reflections of climatic and other natural causes, which may not be changed through subsequent processing.[5] Thus, comparisons of quality across developed and developing countries are relevant for manufactured goods for which there is scope for substantial transformations of the attributes of the basic inputs. If we look at the range of quality indices in the four panels in Figure 1, it clearly brings out the stark gap in the quality of manufactured goods between the rich and developed North and the less-developed South. Panel (a) reveals that the quality indices for Australia, Japan and the UK were at par with those of the United States in the 1960s and early 1970s, but thereafter, while Japan produced marginally better-quality manufactured goods than the United States, Australia and the UK fell behind. On the other hand, for low-income countries such as the four African countries reported in panel (d), as well as for lower-middle-income countries such as India, Indonesia, Morocco and Sri Lanka, as reported in panel (c), lower

---

[4] We consider the United States to be the benchmark country for comparing the situation in the other countries given that the United States has been a consistent producer and exporter of high-quality products with its average quality (aggregate) index always among the top three during the entire period of analysis (1962–2014).

[5] For example, tea grown in India or Sri Lanka and coffee beans grown in Uganda may be of better quality than tea and coffee beans grown elsewhere.

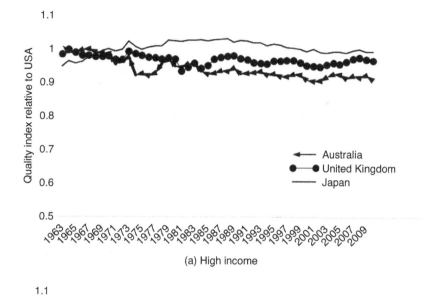

(a) High income

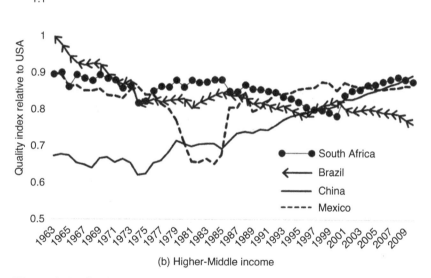

(b) Higher-Middle income

Figure 1 Quality indices of manufactured goods relative to those of the USA
(1963–2010)

Source: Authors' calculation based on IMF data, 2014 (www.imf.org/external/np/res/
dfidimf/diversification.htm).

average quality of manufactured exports is evident. Of course, low-income
countries lag behind to a larger extent than lower-middle-income countries.
However, the striking similarity among these four low-income countries is that
the quality levels of their manufactured goods have worsened steadily since the
late 1970s. In contrast, India, Indonesia and Sri Lanka have improved the quality

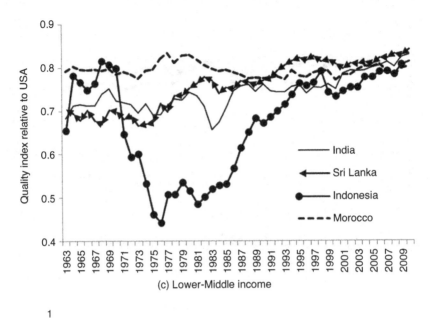

(c) Lower-Middle income

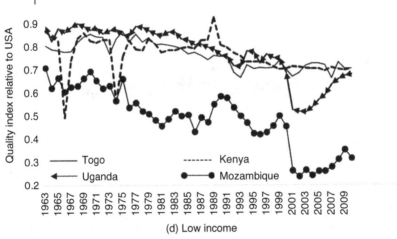

(d) Low income

Figure 1 (cont.)

of their manufactured goods since the late 1970s, with quality upgrading being most spectacular in Indonesia, although the average quality of the manufactured exports of these countries remains well below that of the United States and other rich countries. An interesting observation that we can make here is that Uganda produced better-quality manufactured goods, on average, than all these four lower-middle-income countries during the 1960s and 1970s. Lower average quality for the four upper-middle-income countries – Brazil, China, Mexico and

South Africa – is reported in panel (b). The quality of Brazil's manufactured goods deteriorated steadily after the 1960s and by 2008 had fallen to the level of quality produced by India, Indonesia and Sri Lanka. China has achieved remarkable improvement since the early 1990s, catching up with South Africa by the late 1990s and with Mexico by 2005.

2.3 Asymmetric Quality Variations

In addition to the non-monotonic movements in average quality among the developing countries presented in Figure 1, a deeper look into the data also reveals asymmetric variations in quality across some export product groups for some of the developing countries. A first-hand and somewhat crude indicator of asymmetric quality variations is the pair-wise correlation value. A positive correlation value for a pair of products during a particular time interval suggests that their quality levels have moved mostly in tandem (or in the same direction). A negative correlation value, on the other hand, indicates that quality variations have been asymmetric for the concerned pair of product groups.

The correlation tables below exemplify the quality variations across five product groups for several countries from different income groups. In line with the technological explanation of Ganguly and Acharyya (2021), the five product groups (at the SITC two-digit level) considered for each country are a sample of product groups with different factor intensity requirements for their respective quality upgrading. For example, while higher-quality medicinal and pharmaceutical products (MPP) and chemical elements and compounds (CC) are relatively more skill intensive than they are capital intensive, higher-quality transport equipment (TE) and electrical machinery, appliances and apparatus (EM) require more capital than skilled labour. On the other hand, petroleum and petroleum products (PPP) are largely imported input intensive in most countries.

Tables 1 and 2 report correlations in quality across these five product groups for Japan and the United States, respectively, calculated for the period 1980–2000. While significant negative correlation values can be observed only between product groups PPP and MPP, and between TE and MPP for the United States, such asymmetric variations are completely absent in the case of Japan. Similar absence (or very few cases) of asymmetric variations has been recorded for other high-income countries such as the UK and Australia. This is indicative of the link between the level of development of a country and its gradual attainment of quality convergence, which was also pointed out by Henn et al. (2013).

Table 1 Correlations in product quality levels for Japan (1980–2000)

	PP	CC	MPP	EM	TE
PPP	1				
CC	0.5263*	1			
MPP	0.3846	0.5488*	1		
EM	0.1515	0.5841*	0.0223	1	
TE	-0.2407	-0.0312	0.1237	0.1132	1

Table 2 Correlations in product quality levels for the USA (1980–2000)

	PP	CC	MPP	EM	TE
PPP	1				
CC	-0.2634	1			
MPP	0.4997*	-0.0098	1		
EM	0.1963	0.3898	-0.1960	1	
TE	0.2677	0.5559*	-0.4502*	0.3802	1

Note: Values with an asterisk (*) indicate statistical significance at 95% confidence interval.
Source: Authors' calculations using Stata-13.

Table 3 shows the case of a high-middle-income country, Brazil. In the period for which the correlation values are calculated, asymmetric quality variations across product groups are found to be more pronounced and significant. Further, TE has moved in the opposite direction with respect to all four of the other categories. It is interesting to note that this period of study also coincides with the commencement of the 1980 Debt Crisis in Latin America. The lost decade of development for the debt-ridden countries therein is reflected in highly diverging and irregular quality movements across product groups for Mexico and Argentina as well.

However, China's situation was quite different from that of the other high-middle-income countries, as mentioned earlier. Positive and significant correlation values can be observed for all pairs of product groups in Table 4 from the mid-1980s till 2010, indicating no dissimilar cross-product quality variations whatsoever. This is also the same timeline during which China started pushing up its aggregate quality levels to catch up with high-quality-producing countries like the United States (see Figure 1, panel (b)).

As one goes down the ladder of development, coming to the lower-middle-income countries, evidence of asymmetric quality variations varies across

Table 3 Correlations in product quality levels for Brazil (1980–2010)

	PP	CC	MPP	EM	TE
PPP	1				
CC	0.5492*	1			
MPP	0.5888*	0.6227*	1		
EM	0.7349*	0.7123*	0.7740*	1	
TE	-0.5895*	-0.4197*	-0.7542*	-0.5489*	1

Table 4 Correlations in product quality levels for China (1985–2010)

	PP	CC	MPP	EM	TE
PPP	1				
CC	0.5203*	1			
MPP	0.5603*	0.9826*	1		
EM	0.5924*	0.9284*	0.9186*	1	
TE	0.5605*	0.9430*	0.9479*	0.8877*	1

countries. Line graphs for Indonesia (Figure 2) and the Philippines (Figure 3) show that while both were similarly and adversely hit by the financial contagion in Asia in the late 1990s, significant asymmetric quality variations are present in the former country but almost absent from the latter.

The trends mapped here show that quality levels of CC, TE and MPP move opposite to each other during almost the entire period of study for Indonesia with statistically significant negative correlation values: -0.5557 between CC and MPP, and -0.3939 between CC and TE. On the other hand, significant positive correlation between these very product groups – 0.4739 between CC and MPP, 0.4424 between TE and CC – is observed for the Philippines, also captured through quality lines that move in tandem with each other. All of this suggests that the trade, globalisation and development policies adopted by these countries during 1985–2010 had asymmetric effects on the quality of export goods across different product categories.

In the case of India, another developing low-middle-income country, trends in asymmetric quality variations have been observed across a different set of product groups. Such asymmetric variations are more pronounced after the mid-1980s, which marks the beginning of the liberalisation of import of capital and intermediate goods by India. As documented in Ganguly and Acharyya (2022a),

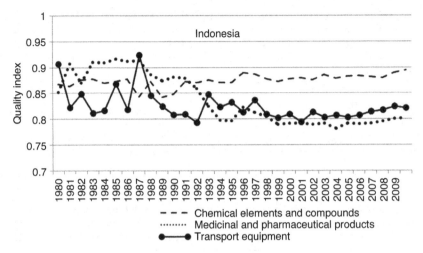

Figure 2 Quality variations: Indonesia
Source: Authors' calculation based on IMF data, 2013.

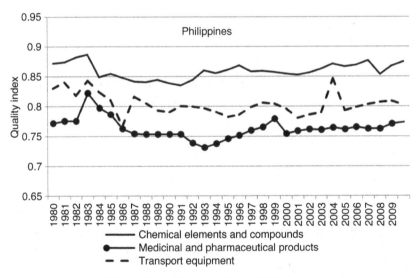

Figure 3 Quality variations: Philippines
Source: Authors' calculation based on IMF data, 2013.

significant negative correlation between EM and non-ferrous metals (-0.5944), between non-ferrous metals and MPP (-0.7302), and between leather manufactures and plastic materials (-0.7447) could be observed. Similar trends have been observed with leather manufactures, PPP, MPP, CC, and EM during that period.

Table 5 Correlations in product quality levels for Uganda (1980–2000)

	PP	CC	MPP	EM	TE
PPP	1				
CC	0.344	1			
MPP	-0.5739*	-0.0371	1		
EM	0.1434	0.2873*	0.1447*	1	
TE	-0.1299*	-0.1081*	0.381	0.3918	1

Finally, coming to the low-income countries, Uganda, being one of the largest merchandise exporters to high-income countries (per the World Development Indicators 2013 Bank database), exhibits even more profound asymmetric quality variation among these product groups (see Table 5). Extending the period of analysis by a further ten years retains this dimension of asymmetric quality variations.

These observations suggest that trade liberalisation policies adopted by countries at different points during the wave of globalisation may have affected the quality of their export goods asymmetrically. Export-promotion strategies such as tariff reductions raise the prices of some domestic inputs while lowing the prices of a few others. This may have differential effects on the choice of quality of export products, which varies from one product to another with respect to the skill or capital intensities required for higher-quality varieties.

To conclude, quality estimates developed by Henn et al. (2013) fill in the gap in the quality estimation literature where cross-country comparisons, especially those incorporating developing countries, could not be made using country-specific estimation procedures in different studies. Using such estimates, we document the stark gap in the quality of manufactured goods between the rich and developed North and the less-developed South, as well as asymmetric quality variations across different product categories.

3 Explaining the Low (Export) Quality Phenomenon: Theory and Empirics

The existing literature provides alternative explanations for the low-export-quality phenomenon in developing countries in terms of demand factors, supply factors – technology, endowment and market structure – and trade as well as domestic policies. Often the supply factors and policies are intertwined. For example, restrictive trade policies, like import quotas (or prohibitively high tariffs), allow domestic monopolies to exercise market power by restricting entry of foreign firms, which influences their choices of product quality and also the innovation level. Similarly, as trade policies cause some sectors to expand and others to contract under full employment of some (or all) of the domestic resources, they can affect the cost of quality by changing the factor prices in consequence, and accordingly incentivise or disincentivise quality upgrading. The nature of the good under consideration also matters. For goods whose quality cannot be judged by the buyers a priori – 'experience goods', in the terminology of Nelson (1974) – there is asymmetric information regarding product quality available to buyers, which may discourage a producer from producing a quality that is higher than the buyers' perception of the average industry quality. In the case of traded goods, buyers' perception of the country of origin of the goods imported matters, especially when goods are coming from developing countries.

In this section we discuss the alternative explanations in terms of demand and supply fundamentals, setting aside discussion of the role of trade and industrial policy until Section 4. We begin with the demand-side explanations that focus on consumer heterogeneity – both within and across countries – in terms of taste diversity and/or income disparity influencing quality choices by firms.

3.1 Demand-Side Explanations

Demand-side explanations for low product quality date back to the three pioneering analyses of quality choices by firms in a partial equilibrium framework by Mussa and Rosen (1978), Gabszewicz and Thisse (1979) and Shaked and Sutton (1982). A substantial literature followed these groundbreaking works that demonstrated quality discrimination and under-provision of quality by a monopolist as well as quality differentiation by oligopolistic firms when consumers are heterogeneous with respect to their tastes or incomes. There is also a small and relatively newer general equilibrium analysis relating income disparities and distribution to quality from the demand side (Fajgelbaum, Grossman and Helpman, 2011). In Sections 3.1.1 and 3.1.2, we briefly discuss these two literatures and their implications for the low-export-quality phenomenon in developing countries.

3.1.1 Income Disparities and Quality Variations: Partial Equilibrium Analysis

The central theme of the partial equilibrium endogenous quality choice models is that when buyers can observe quality a priori, such as in the case of search goods, their marginal willingness to pay (MWP) increases with the level of quality of the good under consideration. This, along with the marginal cost of production increasing with the quality level, determines the profit-maximising quality provided by firms from a set of technologically feasible quality levels. So, for any given cost of quality, if MWP in a market is low, the quality offered will be low as well. Low incomes of consumers in developing countries can also cause their purchasing power (PP) constraint to be binding and thus can cause firms to provide a lower quality than they would otherwise (Acharyya, 2005). Thus, cross-country income differences can explain the low-export-quality phenomenon in developing counties, with or without a (binding) PP constraint. Furthermore, when consumers are heterogeneous, firms discriminate among them by offering different pairs of prices and qualiy levels. This can result in further quality degrading in the developing country.

These implications of cross-country as well as within-country income and demand disparities for the low-export-quality phenomenon of exports by low-income developing countries can be explained as follows. Let $Q \in [0, 1]$ denote the index of observable quality. A consumer buys, if at all, only one unit of the good, which is a standard assumption employed in the literature intended to separate out quality and quantity dimensions of demand.[6] This also enables us to focus solely on a consumer's choice regarding whether to buy a quality-differentiated good, and, if so, which particular quality to buy, from among the different qualities of the good available in the market. Such a decision over the quality dimension of a good – that is, whether to buy and which quality to buy, instead of how much to buy – is driven by the marginal utility (MU) that a consumer derives from a particular level of quality Q net of the unit price that she pays.[7] Higher utility from consuming a better-quality good makes her MWP increase with the quality of the good. The MWP also depends on the type of the consumer. If she is a high type – having either better taste or higher income than another buyer – then she derives larger additional utility from consuming a better quality than other (low-type) buyers and, therefore, is willing to pay *more* for it. However, to begin with, suppose all buyers in each country are identical in all respects, so that all consumers derive the same MU from a better quality of the good under consideration and thus pay the same additional price for it.

Suppose in each country the good is produced by perfectly competitive firms. Due to higher MWP by a (representative) consumer for a better quality, each firm can get a larger revenue by offering a better quality. But producing a higher quality entails larger costs – both total and marginal costs. Under the simplify-ing assumption that the marginal cost (MC) of production is invariant with

---

[6] Gabszewicz and Wauthy (2002) is the one exception that considered a consumer deciding about buying a discrete number of units of the good.

[7] The literature assumes that the marginal utility of money income is constant and is normalised to unity.

respect to the number of units of the good being produced, although it is larger for a better quality, the profit-maximising quality that each competitive firm will offer will be the one for which the MWP equals the MC.

Now, to focus on how the cross-country disparity in (per capita) income levels explains the low-export-quality phenomenon in a developing (or poor) country, let the MWP depend on the income level, as in Gabszewicz and Thisse (1979), for example. Let y denote the income level of a representative consumer in the developing country. Let P be the price of the good in the local market. Then, the net utility V derived by the representative consumer from consuming the good of quality Q at the price P is given by:

$$V(y, Q, P) = U(y, Q) - P, \quad U_y > 0, \ U_Q > 0, \ U_{QQ} < 0 \tag{1}$$

where U represents the gross utility. The first partial derivative in Equation (1) indicates that the representative consumer's utility increases with her income level (or her *type*) for any given Q; the other two partial derivatives indicate that her utility increases with the quality of the good at a decreasing rate, *given her type*. Essentially, the MU from quality variation, U_Q, is her MWP for quality. An important property of the net utility function in Equation (1) deserves attention: it is additively separable in quality and price. This makes the upward-sloping iso-net-utility curves in the (Q, P) space, or the indifference curves between price and quality, *vertically parallel* to each other. This has some far-reaching implications, as we will discuss later. Given that her reservation utility is zero, the consumer buys the good if and only if her net utility $V(a, Q, P)$ is non-negative.[8] This defines her individually rational (IR) or the market participation (MP) constraint.

Let there be a richer developed country with all consumers being identical there as well. They have the same utility functions and their purchase decisions are also the same as the consumers in the developing country, but they have a higher (per capita) income, y^*. By the specification of the gross utility function in Equation (1), therefore, the consumers in the low-income developing country derive lower total as well as marginal utilities than the consumers in the richer country:

$$U(y, Q) < U(y^*, Q), \quad U_Q(y, Q) < U_Q(y^*, Q) \tag{2}$$

Suppose competitive firms in both the countries are identical in terms of technology – including knowledge about the feasible set of qualities – and

---

[8] If $V = 0$, the consumer is indifferent between buying and not buying the good (or the menu (P, Q)), and the tie-breaking rule applied in the literature is that in case of indifference she *buys* the good.

costs. Let the MC of producing the good, c, be invariant with respect to the output level but increasing in the quality level at an increasing rate:

$$c = c(Q), \; c_Q > 0, \; c_{QQ} > 0 \tag{3}$$

It is then straightforward to check that, under autarchy, quality levels Q_C and Q_C^* will be provided by the competitive firms in the low-income country and the rich country, respectively, such that

$$U_Q(y, Q_C) = c_Q(Q_C), \; U_Q(y^*, Q_C^*) = c_Q(Q_C^*) \tag{4}$$

By the property of the utility function and that of the cost function, it immediately follows that $Q_C < Q_C^*$. Thus, low (per capita) income explains the low-export-quality phenomenon in the developing country. This is illustrated in Figure 4. The upward-sloping concave curves represent the indifference curves between price and quality for representative consumers in the two countries: The steeper (broken) curve is that for a consumer in the rich country and the flatter (solid) curve is that for a consumer in the low-income developing country. Curves labelled $V^* = 0$ and $V = 0$ represent the IR constraints. The upward-sloping convex curve represents the identical MC function specified in Equation (3). The first-order conditions in Equation (4) are satisfied at E_C and E_C^*. The net utilities derived by the consumers in the two countries are indicated by the curves labelled V_C and V_C^*. These curves being strictly below the IR constraints means that the consumers in each country enjoy strictly positive surpluses at the competitive (autarchic) equilibrium.

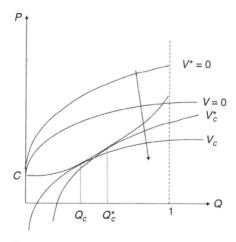

Figure 4 Cross-country quality variations

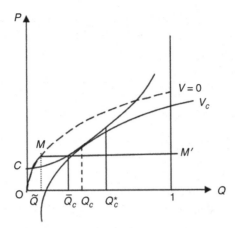

Figure 5 Purchasing power constraint

Low income of consumers in developing countries may also imply that their purchasing power (PP) constraint is binding in the sense that some technologically feasible high-quality varieties, if offered in the market, may not be affordable to them because of the high prices of those varieties. If such a binding PP constraint does not allow the consumers to purchase even the competitive quality Q_C, then firms will provide an even lower quality. To illustrate in the simplest possible manner, let a representative consumer in the developing country spend β fraction of her income on the quality-differentiated good and the remainder on the other goods. If β is low, or y is very low, it may be possible that $\beta y < P_C = c(Q_C)$, in which case the PP constraint is binding. So this may further lower the quality level offered by firms in the developing country.[9] This is illustrated in Figure 5. The MP constraint is now the kinked curve OMM′. For all $Q < \tilde{Q}$ the IR constraint is binding and thus represents the MP constraint. For all other higher qualities, the PP constraint is binding and thus determines the decision to participate in the market and purchase the good. The competitive firms will now offer the quality $\overline{Q}_C$, which is lower than the Q_C that they would have offered without the binding PP constraint.

How do the results change when income disparities exist among consumers in each country? By the property of the utility function specified earlier, the MU from quality in each country will be higher for a richer consumer and thus she will be willing to pay a higher price than a poorer consumer in her country for

---

[9] Acharyya (2005) demonstrates how such a PP constraint per se can explain the low-export-quality phenomenon by considering the case of identical MWP because of identical taste of consumers everywhere. There being cross-country income disparities with the PP constraint binding only for the developing country then explains cross-country quality variations and the consequent low-export-quality phenomenon in the developing country.

a better quality. This heterogeneity enables firms, competitive or otherwise, to offer different price–quality menus to different consumers if the technologically feasible set of qualities is known to all firms without any additional costs.[10] Thus, in each country more than one quality of the good will be offered at the equilibrium.

To illustrate, without any loss of generality, consider the discrete case of only two income levels in each country: consumers with income levels y_H and y_L in the developing country ($y_H > y_L$); and consumers with income levels y_H^* and y_L^* in the rich country ($y_H^* > y_L^*$). The competitive firms in the developing country will offer two distinctively different qualities, Q_{HC} and Q_{LC}, to the rich and poor buyers there, such that

$$U_Q(y_H, Q_{HC}) = c_Q(Q_{HC}), \ \ U_Q(y_L, Q_{LC}) = c_Q(Q_{LC}) \tag{5}$$

Again, by the property of the utility and cost functions, $Q_{HC} > Q_{LC}$. Similarly, competitive producers in the rich country will offer two distinctively different qualities, Q_{HC}^* and Q_{LC}^*, to the rich and poor buyers there, such that

$$U_Q(y_H^*, Q_{HC}^*) = c_Q(Q_{HC}^*), \ \ U_Q(y_L^*, Q_{LC}^*) = c_Q(Q_{LC}^*) \tag{6}$$

These choices in each country can be illustrated in the same way as in Figure 4 by reinterpreting cross-country income variations as within-country income disparities. That is, we can interpret the steeper (broken) upward-sloping concave curves as representing the iso-net-utility curves for a representative high-income consumer in each country, and the flatter (solid) curves as representing the iso-net-utility curves for a representative low-income consumer in each country.

A few observations are in order. First, high-income buyers in each country will not mimic low-income buyers. For the developing country, for example, high-income buyers will buy the menu $\{P_H = c(Q_{HC}), Q_{HC}\}$ targeted for them rather than the menu $\{P_L = c(Q_{LC}), Q_{LC}\}$ targeted for the poorer buyers there because it gives them strictly higher net utility. Note, when more than one menu is offered in the market, each buyer must also decide which menu to buy. The high-income buyers will buy menu $\{P_H, Q_H\}$ instead of menu $\{P_L, Q_L\}$ if:

$$V(y_H, P_H, Q_H) \geq V(y_H, P_L, Q_L) \tag{7}$$

---

[10] In contrast to this subset of the literature that assumes the existence of a technologically feasible set of qualities, a parallel subset of the literature considers development of qualities of a good through innovation or research and development (R&D). The firms choose the levels of quality to be developed by incurring a sunk R&D cost prior to deciding what price to charge and which types of buyer to cater to. In such a context, despite consumers being heterogeneous, a firm may develop only one quality to minimise the sunk R&D costs and then may not serve the low-income consumers, an outcome known as partial market coverage.

This is called the incentive compatibility (IC) or self-selection (SS) constraint. The tie-breaking rule applied here is that if a buyer is indifferent between the two menus, $V(y_H, P_H, Q_H) = V(y_H, P_L, Q_L)$, she buys the menu that offers a higher quality. From Figure 4, it can be easily checked that the above IC (or SS) constraint is satisfied for the high-income buyer as a strict inequality for the optimum quality levels Q_{HC} and Q_{LC} defined in Equation (5).

Second, if $y_L < y_L^*$ and $y_H < y_H^*$, then by Equations (5) and (6), $Q_{LC} < Q_{LC}^*$ and $Q_{HC} < Q_{HC}^*$. In such a case, we have quality degradation for all buyers in the low-income developing country that again explains the low-export-quality phenomenon there. Finally, as in the case of identical consumers, in this case of heterogeneous consumers the PP constraint may be relevant for explaining the low-export-quality phenomenon.

3.1.2 Quality Uncertainty, Asymmetric Information and the Lemons Problem

For many goods, particularly durables, consumers cannot judge their quality before purchase. Rather, they have to 'experience' the quality. In such cases of asymmetric information, buyers pay according to their perceptions of the average industry quality. Thus, producers have no incentive to provide a high quality. As long as cost increases with quality, they would prefer to save cost by providing a lower quality. In addition to this moral hazard problem, there can also be an adverse selection when a producer decides whether to put a good in the market for sale or to keep it for self-consumption. Again, since a good of higher quality than the average industry quality cannot be recognised by the consumers because of its unobservable quality, the producer will generally put into the market only goods of lower quality. Bad quality thus drives out good quality from the market. This is what Akerlof (1970) termed the lemons problem in the context of the market for used cars in the United States. These moral hazard and adverse selection issues can explain the low-export-quality phenomenon in developing countries if buyers there perceive the average industry quality to be poorer than in a richer country.[11]

3.1.3 Within-Country Income Distribution and Quality Choice: General Equilibrium Analysis

Among the few general equilibrium analyses of the non-homothetic preferences of consumers and the income disparities among them, the home-market effect in Fajgelbaum et al. (2011) explains why richer countries export higher-quality

---

[11] Asymmetry in the warranty system and in buyers having private information are plausible reasons. See, for example, Tirole (1988) and Acharyya (2005).

goods. This is similar to the Linder (1961) hypothesis that a country produces goods according to the tastes (or demand) of their local consumers and sells to countries with similar tastes or demand patterns. To explain, they considered two countries, Rich and Poor, which have identical technology and factor endowments but different size and distribution of their labour forces. Each country produces two types of good, a homogeneous good, which serves as the numeraire, and a set of differentiated products. Both types of good are produced only by labour. One unit of labour is required to produce one unit of the homogeneous good. On the other hand, similar to Krugman (1979), the differentiated products, which have both variety and quality dimensions, require fixed units of labour per variety as well as per unit of output. Whereas the homogeneous good is produced under competitive conditions, the differentiated goods are produced by monopolistically competitive producers.

Each country has a continuum of individuals endowed with different amounts of labour, and consequently with different wage incomes.[12] That is, heterogeneity in endowments generates a distribution of income. Each individual h consumes the homogeneous good and her optimal choice of variety and quality from the set of differentiated products. Individual varieties of the differentiated product reflect attributes of the product other than its quality. Her utility function displays complementarity between the quantity of the homogeneous good and the quality of the differentiated product as well as an idiosyncratic taste component that captures her valuation of the attributes of the differentiated products:

$$u_j^h = xQ + \varepsilon_j^h \tag{8}$$

where u_j^h is the utility that she derives by consuming x units of the homogeneous good and one unit of variety j of the differentiated product with quality Q; and ε_j^h is her evaluation of the particular attributes of variety j. The complementarity property of this utility function implies a higher MU from a particular quality for those who consume more of the homogeneous good, which in turn implies two things. First, aggregate demand is non-homothetic. Second, since the individual h spends her residual income $y^h - p_j$ on the homogeneous good after buying one unit of her most preferred variety of the differentiated product at the price p_j, so the MU from quality is increasing in her income similar to the specifications of Gabszewicz and Thisse (1979) and Shaked and Sutton (1982).

A firm that produces a variety j with quality q of the differentiated product, using f_q units of labour to develop the variety and c_q units of labour per unit of output of quality q, earns profit equal to $\pi_j = (p_j - c_q)d_j - f_q$, where d_j is the

---

[12] The wage rate in each country is equal to one at the equilibrium by the above set of assumptions.

aggregate demand for variety j. The profit-maximising price set by the firm is then shown to be a mark-up over the (constant) MC, c_q, with the mark-up differing for goods of different quality.

Given this set-up, trade will be governed entirely by demand differences: either differences in the size of labour forces allowing for different income levels or distribution of labour forces generating differences in distribution of incomes. Assuming that the differentiated products are costly to trade, Fajgelbaum et al. (2011) established the following results. First, under autarchy, there is a larger number of firms producing high-quality goods than there are firms producing low-quality products in the larger country. The opposite holds for the smaller country. Second, asymmetry in the relative number of firms producing high-quality goods in the two countries carries over to free trade with incomplete specialisation. Third, similar results hold when the two countries are identical in size but the distribution in the richer country first-order stochastically dominates that in the poorer country. This is because a more dispersed distribution of income in the richer country results in a larger home demand for high-quality goods and a smaller home demand for low-quality goods. More firms then enter the market to produce high-quality goods in the more unequal richer country.

From these results it follows that the richer country will be a net exporter of higher-quality goods and a net importer of lower-quality goods. This, as Fajgelbaum et al. (2011, p. 724) exemplify, explains 'why Germany tradition-ally has exported high-quality cars to Korea while importing low-quality cars from there'.

3.2 Supply-Side Explanations: Technology, Factor Endowment and Cost of Quality

Supply-side explanations of the low-export-quality phenomenon in developing countries include market structure (or nature of entry and competition among firms), technology and costs. In Section 3.2.1 we discuss the role of market structure in the context of the partial equilibrium endogenous quality choice models discussed in Section 3.1.1. The contestable nature of markets in the developing countries with hit-and-run entry is another plausible explanation of the low-export-quality phenomenon that we discuss in Section 3.2.2. Technology determines the costs of quality and consequently provision of quality. This aspect of cross-country technology asymmetry as an explanation is discussed in Section 3.2.3. In this context, general equilibrium analyses following Falvey and Kierzkowski (1987), Flam and Helpman (1987), Acharyya and Jones (2001) and Ganguly and Acharyya (2020, 2021), among others, allow us to focus on the endogeneity of costs of quality in contrast to exogenously given costs in the partial equilibrium models. Such analyses also enable us to relate the low-export-quality phenomenon to scarcity of domestic factors of production in the developing countries.

3.2.1 Monopoly, Patents and Under-Provision of Quality

Consider the benchmark analysis of Section 3.1.1 where consumers in each country have the same income level (as well as tastes) and thus have the same MWP but have a lower income level if they belong to a developing country than if they belong to a rich country. The same low-export-quality phenomenon derived in such a context arises if domestic monopolies, instead of competitive firms, provide the good under autarchy, which segments the national markets. In fact, the domestic monopolies will offer the *same* qualities as the competitive firms:

$$Q_m = Q_C < Q_C^* = Q_m^* \; \forall \; y < y^* \tag{9}$$

This follows from the vertically parallel property of the iso-net-utility curves mentioned earlier.[13]

But, in each country the domestic monopolist will charge the maximum price that the consumers will be willing to pay for that level of quality, as given by their IR constraint, and thus extract all the surpluses from them by leaving them with zero net utility. In other words, under monopoly provision of the quality-differentiated good and with identical consumers in each country, there will be price distortion only, with no quality distortion. So, up to this point, market structure or monopoly provision of quality does not add any new dimension to the low-export-quality phenomenon.

However, if we consider the case of within-country income disparities and thus heterogeneous consumers in each country, then monopoly provision of quality will have some additional implications. Two results are particularly relevant for our present discussion. First is that a monopolist may not cater to all consumers depending on the within-country distribution of consumers; second is that there will be *under-provision of quality* by a monopolist when it caters to all with a separating (or different price–quality) menu.

To illustrate, consider again the discrete case of only two types of buyer in each country as specified earlier. Let the number of consumers having these income levels be, respectively, n_H, n_L, n_H^* and n_L^*. As shown in Acharyya (1998, 2005), the monopolist will serve both buyers in the developing country with

---

[13] See Acharyya (2005) for a formal proof.

a separating menu – two distinctly different price–quality pairs – if the number of poor buyers is sufficiently large in the following sense:

$$\frac{n_L}{n_H} > \frac{U_Q(y_H, Q_L) - U_Q(y_L, Q_L)}{U_Q(y_L, Q_L)} \tag{10}$$

If the poorer buyers are also served by a menu $\{P_L = U(y_L, Q_L), Q_L\}$ that extracts all surpluses from them, the monopolist must offer high-income buyers a menu $\{P_H, Q_H\}$ that satisfies their IC constraint in Equation (7) as a strict equality, which will leave them with some positive surpluses. That is, while the monopolist gains some profit by catering to the low-income buyers, it loses some profit by not being able to extract all surpluses from the high-income buyers as a consequence. Note that this loss arises because the monopolist does not know which buyers are high-income buyers and, even if it had known, it cannot segment the market to prevent arbitrage among low-income and high-income buyers. Thus, the number of low-income buyers must be sufficiently large to compensate for the loss of profit incurred by catering to them. This critical mass of low-income buyers relative to the mass of high-income buyers is given by the right-hand-side value in Equation (10), which indicates the extent to which the MWP of the high-income buyers exceeds the MWP of the low-income buyers in the developing country. If this condition is not satisfied, then the monopolist caters only to the high-income buyers by offering the menu $\{P_H = U(y_H, Q_{HM}), Q_{HM}\}$, thereby extracting all surpluses from them, where $Q_{HM} = Q_{HC}$. This is the case of partial market coverage.

In the case of full market coverage, that is, for income distribution satisfying the condition in Equation (10), while the richer buyers will still be offered the same quality as under partial market coverage (and as provided by the competitive firms), the poorer buyers will be offered a lower quality than the competitive firms: $Q_{LM} < Q_{LC}$. This result is known as under-provision of quality by a monopolist, or *quality distortion at the bottom*. It arises because by degrading quality for poorer buyers, the monopolist can charge the high-income buyers a higher price and thus can extract a larger surplus from them than it could if it had offered the poorer buyers the same quality as the competitive firms. To what extent the quality will be degraded or under-provided, however, will depend on the mass of poor buyers. The smaller they are in number, the larger will be the quality degradation or the extent of under-provision of quality. At the extreme, when they are very small in number in the sense of reverse inequality in Equation (10), they will not be served at all, whereas the high-income buyers will be charged the maximum price that they are willing to pay for the quality $Q_{HM} = Q_{HC}$.

This under-provision result may explain the low-export-quality phenomenon in many ways. One case is where the rich country market is partially covered – the number of poor buyers there is too small to satisfy the condition similar to Equation (10) – and the developing country market is fully covered – too many low-income buyers there relative to high-income buyers. Another case is where the quality-differentiated good is produced by competitive firms in the rich country and by a monopolist in the developing country.[14] In this case of different market structures, we will have $Q_{LM} < Q^*_{LC}$ and. $Q_{HM} \leq Q^*_{HC}$.[15]

The above results can also explain low quality in the developing country when the quality-differentiated good under consideration is a patented product and is produced and provided by a patent-holder multinational corporation (MNC) in all markets under the patent protection. With no within-country income disparity, the MNC will offer the same pair of menus as the competitive firms (or domestic monopolies under autarchy in the case of a non-patented product) if it can segment the national markets and stop arbitrage across the two markets: a lower quality (with a lower price) to the low-income country and a higher quality with a higher price in the rich country due to income differences. However, if it cannot stop arbitrage by segmenting the markets, then it must ensure that the buyers in the rich country will not buy the menu offered to the buyers in the low-income developing country.[16] That is, it must offer menus that are compatible with the SS or IC constraints of the buyers. And by the under-provision of quality result discussed earlier in the case of within-country income disparity, the MNC will further degrade the quality in the low-income developing country.

3.2.2 Contestable Markets and the Cost of Reputation Building

In markets with repeated purchases of non-durable goods, buyers often judge the unobservable quality and circumvent asymmetric information by drawing from their experiences with the quality of a good purchased from a firm in the past and take that as an indicator of the present or future quality of the same or similar good(s) produced by it. Thus, reputation plays a major role in cases of repeat purchases of non-durables, and, realising it, the firms may like to build

---

[14] Trade and industrial policies in developing countries often restrict entry of firms – domestic as well as foreign – and make the domestic markets far less competitive.

[15] $Q_{HM} < Q^*_{HC}$ if $y_H < y^*_H$ and $Q_{HM} = Q^*_{HC}$ if $y_H = y^*_H$.

[16] An example of failure to stop arbitrage across markets, even for a patented product, is parallel imports of a patented medicine allowed by countries under the Trade-Related Aspects of Intellectual Property Rights flexibility clause of the WTO.

reputation to overcome the moral hazard problem.[17] Note that a higher quality entails higher costs, necessitating that consumers pay a higher price. But, quality being unobservable, consumers can be induced to pay a higher price through building and maintaining reputation (such as by establishing a brand name) and thereby signalling that the firm is a producer of high-quality goods. On the other hand, selling low-quality goods at a higher price at present by exploiting buyers' lack of information regarding the actual quality of the good, a firm may acquire a bad reputation or perception of it that in turn may hurt its sales and profit opportunities in the future.

But gains from building and maintaining reputation are to be realised only in the long run, and thus, unless the future stream of profits is sufficiently large, there will not be much incentive for firms to build reputation. Market structure thus plays an important role here. Most of the markets in developing countries are *contestable* in nature: many small producers; and no sunk costs of operation, making entry and exit free and easy. Whenever a profit opportunity for incumbent firms arises due to, say, a favourable demand shock, *hit-and-run entry* quickly erodes such opportunities. The entrants, being transient in nature, care little about product quality. On the other hand, since in such contestable markets the costs of building and maintaining reputation cannot be recovered through super-normal profits, incumbent firms will have little or no incentive for reputation building and would instead settle for producing low or the average industry quality.[18]

3.2.3 Technology, Factor Endowment and Domestic Factor Cost

The partial equilibrium endogenous quality choice models also bring out the role of technology and costs in many ways, as discussed in Acharyya (2005). One case is that additional costs for higher quality are larger in developing countries than in the richer, more advanced counties due to poor technology there:

$$c(Q) > c^*(Q), c_Q > c_Q^* > 0, \ c_{QQ} > c_{QQ}^* > 0 \quad \forall Q \tag{11}$$

Then, replicating the earlier arguments, it can be seen that even if MWP is the same across all consumers, due to identical per capita income, firms in the technologically backward developing country will offer lower quality than

---

[17] The early works on this dimension were Klein and Leffler (1981), Shapiro (1983) and Allen (1984).

[18] See Rashid (1988) for examples of contestable markets explaining the low quality of clothes in the UK in the pre-Industrial Revolution era and in China in the nineteenth century; adulterated milk and rice mixed with pebbles in many developing countries in the twentieth century, such as Bangladesh and India; and the like.

firms in technologically advanced countries. Moreover, as shown in Acharyya (1998), if the superior technology in advanced countries is such that the MC of quality is either invariant with respect to quality or slowly rising in quality in the sense that for the poorest buyer $U_Q(\underline{y}^*, \overline{Q}) > c_Q(\overline{Q})$, then the topmost quality $\overline{Q}$ will be offered by the firms there.

In general equilibrium, costs are endogenous and depend on the prices of the factors required to produce quality-differentiated goods. If the quality-differentiated goods are produced only by domestic factors like capital and/or skilled labour, then both larger units of such factors required per unit of output – for a particular quality as well as across different quality levels – due to poor technology, and the relative scarcity of such factors in the developing countries result in larger marginal costs for higher qualities.[19] Technological inferiority and factor scarcity thus force them to specialise and produce a range of low qualities compared to the high-quality products produced by the rich and more advanced countries. For example, Flam and Helpman (1987) offer an explanation for such specialisation patterns in terms of Ricardian comparative cost advantages arising from technological differences.[20] Murphy and Shleifer (1997), on the other hand, emphasise the comparative advantage of the richer countries in producing high-quality goods because of the relative abundance of human capital there. Thus, developing countries, being scarce in human capital, produce low-quality goods. A similar factor endowment explanation is offered in Acharyya and Jones (2001) and Ganguly and Acharyya (2021), whereas differences in both factor endowment and technology are emphasised in Falvey and Kierzkowski (1987).

To illustrate the role of technology, as in Flam and Helpman (1987), consider the same set of goods as defined earlier: a homogeneous good, serving as the numeraire, and a continuum of quality-differentiated goods. A consumer with income level y buys her desired quantity x of the homogeneous good but one unit of the desired quality of the differentiated good that maximises her utility $U(x,Q)$ subject to the budget constraint $y \geq x + p(Q)$. The utility function is assumed to display the same complementarity property as discussed earlier. All goods are produced only by labour. While the homogeneous good requires one unit of labour per unit of output, the continuum of quality-differentiated goods indexed by the quality levels $Q \in [0, \overline{Q}]$ require $a(Q)$ and $a^*(Q)$ units of labour per unit of output of

---

[19] The importance of domestic factors such as skilled labour in quality upgrading has been observed by Brambilla et al. (2012, 2014) and Brambilla and Porto (2016). The role of imported input, on the other hand, is highlighted in Kugler and Verhoogen (2012), Bas and Strauss-Khan (2013), Fan and Li (2013) and Hu et al. (2017).

[20] Matsuyama (2000) reasons similarly: In a Ricardian continuum goods model à la Dornbusch et al. (1977), he shows that a high-income North has a comparative advantage in a higher spectrum of goods, and a low-income South has a comparative advantage in a lower spectrum.

quality Q in the developing country and in the advanced country, respectively. These per unit labour requirements, determined by the technology available to the countries under consideration, increase in the quality level; but the *relative* labour requirements, $a(Q)/a^*(Q)$, *decrease* in the quality level. The latter assumption implies that the developing country's comparative advantage *diminishes* as we move from lower- to higher-quality goods. This production structure resembles the one in the Ricardian continuum of goods model à la Dornbusch, Fischer and Samuelson (1977). If the homogeneous good is produced only in the developing country, the wage rate measured in terms of it is equal to one there. Thus, a good of quality $Q_0 \in [0, \overline{Q}]$ is produced in the developing country if $a(Q_0) \leq w^* a^*(Q_0)$ and accordingly the (supply) price of the differentiated good with quality Q is given by:

$$p(Q) = \min[a(Q), w^* a^*(Q^*)] \tag{12}$$

Let $\widetilde{Q} \in [0, \overline{Q}]$ be such that $a(\widetilde{Q}) = w^* a^*(\widetilde{Q})$. Then, by the assumed chain of comparative advantages, the developing country will be producing and supplying low-quality goods in the range $[0, \widetilde{Q}]$, whereas the advanced country produces high-quality goods in the range $[\widetilde{Q}, \overline{Q}]$. Since the assumed chain of comparative advantage underlying this production specialisation along the continuum reflects the inferior technology of the developing country for higher-quality goods, so technological inferiority explains the low-export-quality phenomenon.[21]

In Falvey and Kierzkowski (1987), a slightly different production structure of the quality-differentiated goods brings out the role of factor endowments along with the technology. They allow for cross-country technology differences in production of the homogeneous good but the same technology for producing the continuum of qualities. Whereas the homogeneous good requires b and b^* units of labour (L) in the two countries, the differentiated good of quality Q requires one unit of labour and Q units of capital (K) in both the countries. The K/L ratio is fixed for any given quality but increases in quality: Higher quality of the good requires more of K per unit of output. Thus, whereas the X sector is Ricardian type, displaying cross-country technology differences, the Z sector producing the quality-differentiated good has a Heckscher–Ohlin production structure with identical technology across countries.

---

[21] Consumer heterogeneity in terms of income differences matters only to the extent that it determines the borderline quality at the equilibrium. For example, a certain type of redistribution of income causes the range of qualities produced in the developing country to contract. But the pattern of specialisation in the quality-differentiated goods is still driven by cross-country technology asymmetry, unlike the case in Fajgelbaum et al. (2011).

Perfect competition prevails everywhere so that the zero-profit conditions in the developing country, for example, imply:

$$1 = bw \tag{13}$$

$$p(Q) = w + Qr \tag{14}$$

Full employment conditions are given by:

$$bX + Z = L \tag{15}$$

$$\int_0^1 QZ(Q)dQ = K \tag{16}$$

where X is the output of homogeneous good, $Z(Q)$ is the output of a differentiated good with quality Q and Z denotes the total output of the continuum of quality-differentiated goods taken together. Similar conditions with relevant variables with asterisks describe the rich country specifications.

On the demand side, each consumer demands her preferred quality, which, given the relative prices, is uniquely determined by her income. A consumer with higher income demands a higher quality. Thus, consumers with different incomes buy different qualities. However, unlike Flam and Helpman (1987) and Fajgelbaum et al. (2011), a consumer buys more than one unit of the differentiated good of her desired quality. The utility of a consumer with income y thus depends on the units of the homogeneous good (x) and on both the units and the quality of the differentiated good, z and Q: $U(x, z, Q)$. Given the prices defined earlier, the desired quality and quantities are decided by her by maximising utility subject to the budget constraint $y = x + p(Q)z = xwz + rQz$.

Given these specifications, intra-industry trade in quality-differentiated products will be characterised as follows. Both an inferior technology in the homogeneous product and scarcity of capital would mean that the developing country will be exporting low-quality varieties to the rich country and will import higher-quality varieties from there. To explain, note that, for reasons similar to that spelled out earlier, the post-trade price of a particular quality will be the minimum of the unit cost of production in the two countries:

$$p(Q) = \min[w + Qr, w^* + Qr^*] \ \forall \ Q \tag{17}$$

Consider, for example, the case where the rich country has superior technology for producing the homogeneous good, $b^* < b$, and both countries produce this good under free trade. Thus, the wage rate in the developing country will be lower because of lower marginal productivity than in the advanced country. The wage cost of producing any quality of the differentiated product will thus be smaller in the developing country. If, however, the developing country is capital scarce, then the rate of return to capital will be higher there than in the advanced country, putting it at a capital-cost disadvantage. Since capital intensity rises with the quality of the good, so, beyond a critical level of quality, the capital-cost disadvantage will be more pronounced than the labour-cost advantage of the developing country. That is, the developing country will have comparative cost advantage for all qualities lower than this critical level of quality, $\widetilde{Q}$, and the advanced country will have comparative cost advantage for all qualities lower than this, where:

$$w + \widetilde{Q}r = w^* + \widetilde{Q}r^* \tag{18}$$

This pattern of production specialisation is illustrated in Figure 6. In each country the richer consumers will buy the higher-quality varieties produced by the advanced country and the low-income consumers will buy the lower-quality varieties produced by the developing country. The income disparities explain the existence of demand for all qualities in the continuum and hence intra-industry trade in quality-differentiated goods. But, again, the post-trade specialisation in qualities is determined primarily by supply-side determinants such as technology and factor endowment.

Acharyya and Jones (2001) and Ganguly and Acharyya (2021) differ from Falvey and Kierzkowski (1987) – and also from Flam and Helpman (1987) – in two ways. First, they differentiate between the skill levels required to produce the quality-differentiated goods and the two sets of homogeneous goods – traded and non-traded. Second, they study how redistribution of income across different domestic factors of production, resulting from changes in factor endowment, technology or government policy, can affect export quality.

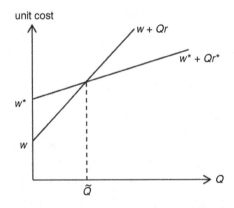

Figure 6 Post-trade production specialisation

They consider a small, open economy where competitive firms select a quality of the differentiated export good from a set of technologically feasible qualities. The world price of this export good, Z, varies positively with the selected quality that reflects the higher MWP of foreign buyers for a better quality of the (imported) good that they consume: $P_Z^W = P_Z^W(Q), P_Z^{W'}(Q) > 0$, $P_Z^{W''}(Q) > 0$. This good is produced by skilled labour (S) and capital in fixed proportion for a particular quality. For a better quality of the good, Acharyya and Jones (2001) assumed a larger per unit requirement of only the capital input:

$$a_{KZ} = a_{KZ}(Q), a'_{KZ}(Q) > 0, a''_{KZ}(Q) > 0 \tag{19}$$

The economy also produces two homogeneous goods – a composite trade good (T) and a non-traded good (N) – using unskilled labour and the same capital as used by export good Z. This (T,N) nugget displays Heckscher–Ohlin–Samuelson properties.[22] Suppose that export good Z is not domestically consumed[23] and that consumers have homothetic (and identical) tastes for the composite traded good and the non-traded good.

Competitive conditions everywhere mean price equals average cost:

$$P_Z^W(Q) = a_{SZ}w_S + a_{KZ}(Q)r \tag{20}$$

$$P_T^W = a_{LT}w + a_{KT}r \tag{21}$$

$$P_N = a_{LN}w + a_{KN}r \tag{22}$$

where, w is the unskilled wage and a_{ij}; $i = S, L, K$; $j = Z, T, N$, denote the per unit requirement of input-i in production of good-j. While a_{SZ} and a_{KZ} are technologically fixed, as mentioned earlier, a_{ij}s in the (T, N) nugget represents the least-cost choices made by the producers that depend only on the wage–rental ratio under the assumption of Constant Returns to Scale (CRS) technology.

For any given rate of return to capital, competitive producers choose the profit-maximising quality $\tilde{Q}$ of Z such that the marginal revenue equals the MC for this quality level:

$$P_Z^{W'}(\tilde{Q}) = a'_{KZ}(\tilde{Q})r \tag{23}$$

---

[22] See Jones (1974) for formalisation of a two-sector model with a composite traded good and a non-traded good. The production structure of the economy as a whole resembles that considered by Gruen and Corden (1970) and subsequently generalised in Jones and Marjit (1992) and Marjit, Ganguly and Acharyya (2020).

[23] This is a simplifying assumption since local demand for traded goods has no relevance in a small, open economy. We will return to this issue in Section 6.

The price of the non-traded good is determined locally and must be the one for which the domestic market clears. Under homothetic tastes, this means:

$$\frac{D_N}{D_T} = f\left(\frac{P_N}{P_T^W}\right) = \frac{X_N}{X_T} \tag{24}$$

where X_T and X_N are output levels of the traded and non-traded goods, respectively.

Finally, flexible factor prices and competition ensure that the domestic factor markets clear as well:

$$\overline{K} - a_{KZ}(Q)X_Z = \widetilde{K}(Q) = a_{KT}X_T + a_{KN}X_N \tag{25}$$

$$\overline{S} = a_{SZ}X_Z \tag{26}$$

$$\overline{L} = a_{LT}X_T + a_{LN}X_N \tag{27}$$

Note that by assuming a fixed per unit requirement of skilled labour for all quality levels, Acharyya and Jones (2001) essentially pin down the output of the quality-differentiated export good Z by the availability of skilled labour.

Referring back to the marginal condition for quality choice shown in Equation (23), note that a ceteris paribus fall in the rate of return to capital lowers the MC at any given level of quality and thus induces firms to upgrade quality. This is captured through the downward-sloping Π_Z curve in Figure 7. On the other hand, a ceteris paribus increase in the export quality raises the demand for capital and thus lowers its availability for the (T, N) nugget. Consequently, similar to the output-magnification effect, the output of the composite traded good falls and that of the non-traded good increases under the assumption that the composite traded good is relatively capital intensive.

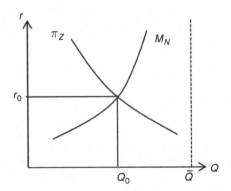

Figure 7 Equilibrium export quality

The non-traded market thus clears at a lower price of the non-traded good, which in turn lowers the unskilled wage and raises the rate of return to capital by the price-magnification effect. This relationship between export quality and rate of return to capital is represented by the positively sloped curve labelled M_N.

The equilibrium quality and the rate of return to capital are thus determined simultaneously corresponding to the point of intersection of these two curves.

The role of factor endowment in explaining the low-export-quality phenomenon is now evident from the previous discussion. A smaller endowment of capital, or alternatively a larger endowment of unskilled labour, means a higher rate of return to capital and correspondingly a higher MC of quality. Competitive firms thus choose a lower quality of the export good Z. That is, relatively unskilled labour-abundant or capital-scarce countries, typically developing countries, will be producers of low-quality export good(s), whereas relatively capital-abundant countries, typically developed countries, will be producers of high-quality export good(s).

In a more generalised case where higher qualities require more of both skilled labour and capital per unit of output, though at different proportions, as considered in Ganguly and Acharyya (2020, 2021), scarcity of skilled labour in developing countries may also explain low quality there. However, the underlying technology for quality upgrading also becomes important. For example, suppose higher-quality varieties require larger units of both capital and skilled labour per unit of output:

$$a_{hZ} = a_{hZ}(Q), \; a'_{hZ}(Q) > 0, \; a''_{hZ}(Q) > 0; \quad h = S, K \tag{28}$$

where a_{hZ} denotes the per unit requirement of input-h.

Thus, the relative capital intensity of a higher-quality variety of good Z can increase or decrease according to the nature of the export good and its technological requirement. More precisely, the relative skill intensity $s_Z = a_{SZ}(Q)/a_{KZ}(Q)$ will increase with 1 per cent betterment of quality if the quality elasticity of the per unit input requirement of skilled labour, γ_{SZ}, is larger than that of capital, γ_{KZ}:

$$\hat{s}_Z = (\gamma_{SZ} - \gamma_{KZ})\hat{Q} > 0 \; \text{if} \; \gamma_{SZ} > \gamma_{KZ} \tag{29}$$

where $\gamma_{hZ} \equiv \frac{Qa'_{hZ}(Q)}{a_{hZ}(Q)} > 0; \quad h = S, K$, and a hat over a variable denotes its proportional change (e.g. $\hat{s}_Z = \frac{ds_Z}{s_Z}$).

The marginal condition Equation (23) now changes to:

$$P_Z^{W'}(\widetilde{Q}) = a'_{SZ}(\widetilde{Q})w_S + a'_{KZ}(\widetilde{Q})r \tag{23a}$$

Since, by the zero-profit condition in Equation (22), the skilled wage and the rate of return vary inversely with each other, so now the Π_Z curve in Figure 7 will be downward sloping only if $\gamma_{SZ} < \gamma_{KZ}$, and positively sloped otherwise.

If $\gamma_{SZ} > \gamma_{KZ}$, that is, *higher qualities are relatively skill intensive*, then a developing country having a smaller endowment of skilled workers, ceteris paribus, will be producing lower qualities of good Z than countries with a relatively larger number of skilled workers.[24]

The differences in technological requirements of quality upgrading for different types of good also explain the asymmetric quality variations across different goods that were reported in Section 2. Ganguly and Acharyya (2021) consider two types of quality-differentiated export good, Z_1 and Z_2, such that $\gamma_{KZ}^1 > \gamma_{SZ}^1$, $\gamma_{KZ}^2 < \gamma_{SZ}^2$. That is, whereas higher-quality varieties of Z_1 are relatively capital intensive, higher-quality varieties of Z_2 are relatively skill intensive. Examples of Z_1-type goods are aerospace products, scientific instruments, defence equipment, household and office equipment, electrical appliances, agro-based products and the like. On the other hand, Z_2 represents goods and services such as software, jewellery, diamond cutting and polishing, IT-enabled services, financial services and the like. Goods Z_1 and Z_2 are produced by skilled labour along with different types of capital. While good Z_1 uses the same type of capital as a homogeneous import-competing good Y, good Z_2 uses a specific type of capital.[25] In such a context, they establish that an increase in the rate of return to capital used by Z_1 and the import-competing good – due to an adverse endowment shock, for example – lowers the quality of good Z_1 and raises the quality of good Z_2.[26] This result follows from the fact that a change in the rate of return to the commonly used capital changes the rate of return to the other type of capital specific to Z_2 production in the same direction but the skilled wage in the opposite direction. Consequently, *at initial quality levels*, changes in the relevant factor prices asymmetrically affect the MC of quality upgrading of Z_1 and Z_2. Thus, with technological requirements for quality upgrading varying across different export goods, capital scarcity may not have adverse implications for the quality of *all* types of export good.

3.3 Concluding Remarks

The central message of the discussion in this section is how fundamentals such as taste diversity, technology and factor endowments can explain both the nature of specialisation by rich and poor countries along the quality

---

[24] In the context of a North–South trade, Das (2003) also demonstrates that the North, being relatively abundant in skilled labour (or, more precisely, having a larger skilled–unskilled labour ratio) compared to the South, will produce higher-quality brands of a good.

[25] Ganguly and Acharyya (2021) consider only traded goods: two types of skill-based quality-differentiated export good, a homogeneous export good produced by unskilled labour (e.g. rice) and a homogeneous import-competing good.

[26] A policy shock such as a reduction of tariff on imports, as considered by Ganguly and Acharyya (2021), can also cause a rise in the rate of return to this type of capital. We will return to this policy shock in Section 4.

spectrum of goods and the observed low-export-quality phenomenon in developing countries. Moreover, under non-homothetic tastes, income disparities both within and across countries – that may itself be a reflection of uneven distribution of factor endowments within a country as well as cross-country differences in such endowments – also cause poorer countries with relatively higher income inequality to emerge as producers of low-quality goods.

Experience goods with unobservable quality and associated information externality, on the other hand, pose an altogether different kind of problem. Foreign buyers rely on firms' reputations and perceptions regarding the country of origin of any imported good that they consume. But the contestable nature of markets in developing countries often creates disincentives for firms there to invest in building and maintaining reputation. Poor country-of-origin perceptions for manufactured goods produced in developing countries also discourage firms there from producing anything of a higher quality than the industry average.

4 Trade Policies, Income Redistribution and Export Quality

Trade and domestic policies can also explain cross-country quality variations. This section focuses on this particular dimension. While direct quality-targeted export-promotion policies (e.g. quality–content production subsidies, subsidising quality certifications to overcome information externalities) may be relevant, it is worthwhile examining what implications traditional trade and exchange rate policies like tariff reductions (regarded as an indirect export-promotion policy) and devaluation may have on export quality. At the same time, since scarcity of skilled labour and/or capital may adversely affect quality choices by exporting firms, allowing factor flows (emigration/immigration and capital inflows) will have some far-reaching impacts on such choices.

4.1 Trade Liberalisation Policies

Tariff liberalisation policies adopted by developed as well as developing countries, ever since their accession to the WTO, are primarily of two types: (1) reduction of tariffs on final import-competing goods and (2) reduction of tariffs on imported inputs. While the significant impact of such tariff cuts on the volume of trade is already recorded in the existing literature, in Sections 4.1.1 and 4.1.2 we analyse their implications for export quality upgrading and consequent gains from trade at the extensive margin.

4.1.1 Tariff Reduction on Final Import Competing Good

It is well known from the celebrated Stolper–Samuelson theorem and its generalisation as the price-magnification effect à la Jones (1965) that reduction of tariff on imported final consumption goods will change domestic factor prices asymmetrically, and accordingly will have income redistribution effects. Given the empirical evidence mentioned in Section 3 regarding higher-quality varieties being dependent on more intensive use of domestic factors such as skilled labour and capital, this would imply two things. First, if relative skill intensity increases with the quality level in the sense defined in Section 3 (see Equation (29)), then a tariff reduction may downgrade export quality if it raises the skilled wage relative to the rate of return to capital. In such a case, tariff reduction fails as an export-quality-promoting strategy. Second, if different goods and services require different technologically fixed relative skill intensities in the upgrading of their respective qualities, then tariff reduction on the imported final goods may lead to asymmetric quality variations across such goods and services.

These results were formally established in Ganguly and Acharyya (2021). Recall the analytical structure outlined in Section 3. The economy produces two quality-differentiated manufactured goods (or services), Z_1 and Z_2, which differ from each other in two ways. First, these goods use different types of capital, K_1 and K_2, respectively, along with skilled labour in production. Second, whereas higher-quality varieties of Z_1 are relatively capital intensive, higher-quality varieties of Z_2 are relatively skill intensive ($\gamma^1_{KZ} > \gamma^1_{SZ}$, $\gamma^2_{KZ} < \gamma^2_{SZ}$). The economy also produces a homogeneous agricultural export good X that is produced by unskilled labour and land, and a homogeneous import-competing good Y produced by unskilled labour and K_1-type capital (which is also used by Z_1). Thus, K_2-type capital and land are specific to the Z_2 and X sectors, respectively. Moreover, in keeping with the observation that labour markets are segmented in most developing countries, Ganguly and Acharyya (2021) assume that while the import-competing good is produced in the formal sector where unskilled workers are paid a (fixed) minimum wage ($\overline{w}$), the agricultural export good is produced in the informal sector where unskilled workers are paid a competitive, market-determined wage.[27] Despite the minimum wage paid in the formal sector, all unskilled workers are fully employed since those who cannot get employed in the formal import-competing

---

[27] The coexistence of formal and informal sectors in developing countries with significant proportions of the total workforce employed in informal sectors is well documented in Marjit (2003), Marjit and Kar (2011) and Bogliaccini (2013). Typically, agriculture has the largest share of informal workers: 85–90 per cent in India, for example.

sector are absorbed in the informal agricultural sector through the necessary fall in unskilled wages there.

In such a set-up, the following zero-profit and marginal conditions help elucidate the relationship between factor prices and export quality:

$$P_{Zm}^W(Q_m) = a_{KZ}^m(Q_m)r_m + a_{SZ}^m(Q_m)w_S \, , \, m = 1, 2 \tag{30}$$

$$P_X^W = a_{LX}w + a_{TX}R \tag{31}$$

$$P_Y = (1 + t)P_Y^W = a_{LY}\overline{w} + a_{KY}r_1 \tag{32}$$

$$P_{Zm}^{W'}(Q_m^0) = a_{KZ}^{m'}(Q_m^0)r_m + a_{SZ}^{m'}(Q_m^0)w_S, \, m = 1, 2 \tag{33}$$

where R is the rate of return to land, $t < 1$ is the rate of ad valorem tariff, and other notations are as specified earlier.

Three observations are in order. First, the quality choices depend only on the two policy parameters – tariff and minimum wage – but not on endowments of two types of capital and skilled labour. Given the fixed minimum wage in the Y sector, the rate of return to K_1-type capital is tied to the tariff-inclusive price of imports P_Y. On the other hand, as evident from Equation (30), given this rate of return to capital, first the skilled wage is determined by the world price of Z_1, and then, given the skilled wage, the rate of return to K_2-type capital is determined by the world price of Z_2. That is, given $\overline{w}$, the rates of return to the two types of capital and the skilled wage are determined solely by the world prices for quality-differentiated goods and the tariff-inclusive price of the import good. Since only these factor prices are relevant for quality choices, the quality levels are independent of endowments. Second, quality variations affect unskilled wage and the return to land by changing the availability of K_1-type capital for the (X, Y) nugget and the output composition there. Although this has some far-reaching implications for income redistribution (or wage inequality), as we will discuss in Section 5, it is itself inconsequential for quality choices. Third, as mentioned in Section 3, whereas r_1 and r_2 move in the same direction in the event of any policy shock, the skilled wage moves in the opposite direction. This is evident from a closer look at Equation (30). Thus, in both quality-differentiated sectors, the skilled labour to capital cost moves uniformly, which sets the stage for asymmetric quality variations due to different technological requirements for improving Q_1 and Q_2.

Now, consider a ceteris paribus reduction in the tariff rate. To begin with, in the formal sector, import-competing production contracts due to increased foreign competition, which lowers demand for both unskilled labour and capital, causing the informal unskilled wage and the rate of return to K_1-type capital

(r_1) to fall. At the initial Q_1, the consequent lower capital cost encourages producers of Z_1 to expand production, which raises both the demand for skilled workers and their wage. Consequent upon this fall in r_1 and rise in w_S, the MC of quality of Z_1 falls because quality upgrading of Z_1 requires more intensive use of capital than skilled labour ($\gamma_{KZ}^1 > \gamma_{SZ}^1$). Producers of Z_1 thus upgrade their quality. On the other hand, at the initial Q_2, the rise in the skilled wage lowers the production of Z_2, which in turn lowers the rate of return to the K_2-type capital specific to this sector. But, since $\gamma_{KZ}^2 < \gamma_{SZ}^2$, the MC of quality rises and producers lower the quality Q_2.

Therefore, reduction of a tariff on imported final consumption goods causes the quality of Z_1 and Z_2 to change asymmetrically and in a contrasting way due to their different technological requirements for domestic inputs for quality upgrading. This provides a plausible explanation of the asymmetric quality variations across different export products as documented in Section 2.

4.1.2 Tariff Reduction on Imported Input

The dependence of production of final traded goods on imported intermediates can be typically observed in many developing countries. Examples of such import inputs are petroleum, oil and lubricants, gold and precious metals for jewellery setting, electrical and electronic components, and CC (chemical elements and compounds). This dependence is partly due to either unavailability of such inputs or lack of good-quality indigenous inputs. High tariffs on imports of inputs and intermediates, put in place in many instances to both drive revenue and protect domestic industries, have compelled domestic producers of final goods to use indigenous inputs and/or imported inputs less intensively, which has adversely affected the quality of such goods. In such a context, it is likely that input-tariff reduction would help domestic producers upgrade the quality of the goods they produce and export, through more efficient use of better-quality imported inputs.

Similarly, since product quality is integral to global value chains (GVCs), then facilitating participation in those through reduction of trade costs such as tariffs and non-tariff barriers (NTBs) may provide an incentive for poorer countries to move up the quality ladder. However, as the GVC Development Report (2017) observes, participation of developing countries in GVCs has been rather limited because only a few have sufficient geographical proximity to the three main interconnected hubs, around the United States, Germany in Europe, and China, Japan and South Korea in Asia. Labour productivity is another reason for the limited participation in GVCs. Thus, quality improvement driven by GVCs may be limited to only a few developing countries.

A sizeable recent empirical literature emphasises the favourable impact of input-trade liberalisation on incentivising quality upgrading of exports. For example, Bas and Strauss-Khan (2013) find that Chinese firms sourcing high-quality inputs from developed countries experience a rise in export prices and upgraded quality of the products they are exporting to the high-income countries. Further, a within-firm quality upgrading of imported inputs after input-trade liberalisation is observed by Bas and Strauss-Khan (2013) as the firms imported not only larger varieties of inputs but also higher-priced inputs. Fan et al. (2018) also observe a causal effect of input-trade liberalisation on quality upgrading in the context of China's accession to the WTO in 2001.

Of course, if the quality and the intensity of use of imported input or intermediate goods were the only key factors for quality upgrading, then input-trade liberalisation incentivising exporters to upgrade the quality of their export goods would be a foregone conclusion. But, once again, the trends in asymmetric quality variations across different product groups discussed in Section 2 speak differently. That reduction of input tariffs may not necessarily improve export quality can be demonstrated in two contexts. First, imported inputs are used in the production of export goods other than quality-differentiated export goods; second, imported inputs are used in the production of quality-differentiated export goods *along with* skilled labour and capital. To demonstrate, recall the analytical structure of Acharyya and Jones (2001) spelt out in Section 3, with the generalised quality-upgrading technology specified in Equation (28) and the corresponding marginal condition in Equation (23a). As a simple extension, suppose the composite traded good uses an imported input (I) in a fixed quantity per unit of output, a_{IT}. This captures the import dependent production in many developing countries. The import of this input at the given world price P_I^W is, however, subject to an advalorem tariff at the rate $\tau < 1$. Thus, the zero-profit condition in Equation (21) in Section 3 should now be rewritten as

$$P_T^W = a_{LT}w + a_{KT}r + a_{IT}(1 + \tau)P_I^W \tag{34}$$

Henceforth, we will refer to this analytical structure as the extended Acharyya–Jones (A–J) framework. For any given input tariff, the export quality and the rate of return to capital are simultaneously determined as before, as re-illustrated in Figure 8. Recall that, for reasons spelt out earlier, the profit-maximising quality choice varies inversely with the rate of return to capital for $\gamma_{SZ} < \gamma_{KZ}$ (as in Figure 8 panel (a)) but positively for $\gamma_{SZ} > \gamma_{KZ}$ (as in Figure 8 panel (b)). Accordingly, the Π_Z curve is downward sloping in the left-hand-side panel and upward sloping in the right-hand-side panel. The other relationship between quality and rate of return to capital, which was depicted through the M_N curve, will also have two different slopes under the generalised quality-upgrading technology. Note that now the output of the quality-differentiated export good Z is no longer pinned down by the availability of skilled labour. So full employment of skilled labour (given by Equation (26)) will become:

$$\overline{S} = a_{SZ}(Q)X_Z \tag{35}$$

Unlike what is represented in Equation (23) earlier, now a ceteris paribus increase in the quality of Z will require not only additional capital but also additional skilled labour, for which output of Z must fall to make such additional skilled workers available for quality upgrading. Consequently, capital demand rises by the extent $\hat{a}_{KZ} = \gamma_{KZ}\hat{Q}$ and falls due to this scale contraction by the extent $\hat{Z} = -\gamma_{SZ}\hat{Q}$ at the margin. Hence, overall, the capital requirement in the production of good Z will rise following quality upgrading if $\gamma_{SZ} < \gamma_{KZ}$, and will fall otherwise. In the latter case, $\gamma_{SZ} > \gamma_{KZ}$, for example, capital released by the Z sector moves to the (T, N) nugget. Assuming that the composite traded good is relatively capital intensive compared to the non-traded good, this larger availability of capital causes output of the composite traded good to rise and that of the non-traded good to fall by the standard output-magnification effect. Consequent excess demand for the non-traded good raises its price. With P_T^W and P_I^W unchanged, this rise in P_N will then raise the unskilled wage and lower the rate of return to capital by the standard price-magnification effect.[28] So a rise in the quality of Z will cause the rate of return to capital to fall when $\gamma_{SZ} > \gamma_{KZ}$, for any given rates of input tariff. Similarly, when a higher-quality variety of Z is relatively more capital intensive ($\gamma_{SZ} < \gamma_{KZ}$), a rise in export quality will raise the rate of return to capital. So the M_N curve is positively sloped if $\gamma_{SZ} < \gamma_{KZ}$ and negatively sloped if $\gamma_{SZ} > \gamma_{KZ}$.

The equilibrium quality Q_0 of the export good/service Z and the rate of return to capital r_0 are thus determined simultaneously at the intersection of the M_N and Π_Z curves for any given rates of input tariff. Now suppose that the tariff on the imported input I is lowered, i.e. $\hat{\tau} < 0$. This raises the effective price received by the producers of the composite traded good, or the effective marginal revenue earned per unit: $(P_T^W - a_{IT}(1+\tau)P_I^W)$. At the initial level of export quality and corresponding P_N, the higher effective price of the composite traded good raises the rate of return to capital (and lowers the unskilled wage) through the price-magnification effect, given the factor intensity assumption that the composite traded good is relatively capital intensive. The M_N curve in both panels in Figure 8 shifts up, causing downgrading of quality if $\gamma_{KZ} > \gamma_{SZ}$ and upgrading if $\gamma_{KZ} < \gamma_{SZ}$.

---

[28] See Jones (1965).

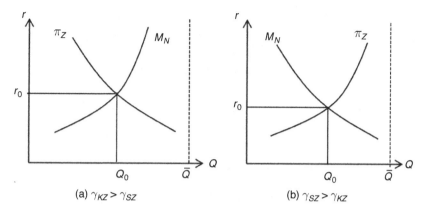

Figure 8 Equilibrium export quality

The case of an imported input being used in the production of a skill-based quality-differentiated good and the impact of a reduction in tariff on this input can similarly be analysed in the extended A–J framework. For example, as shown by Ganguly and Acharyya (2022a), lowering the tariff on the input used in Z good will improve the quality of Z only if a higher-quality variety of it requires additional imported input to a larger extent than additional skilled labour. Reducing the input tariff lowers the MC of quality for any given skilled wage but, at the same time, raises the MC of quality upgrading by raising the skilled wage, since it augments production of skill-based export goods. Hence, overall, the MC of quality will fall, and quality will be upgraded if *relatively* more imported input is required for upgrade quality.

In this context, two recent empirical studies deserve attention. First, Fieler, Eslava and Xu (2018) develop a blended quantitative model of input-trade liberalisation where higher output quality requires both intermediate inputs to be of high quality. If foreign inputs are superior in quality to domestic inputs, then input-trade liberalisation allows monopolistically competitive heterogeneous firms access to higher-quality inputs and endogenously to choose output quality as a function of their productivity, their use of skilled labour and inputs of different quality. Second, Bas and Paunov (2021) show that Ecuador's firms upgraded both the quality of their imported inputs and their skill intensity following input-tariff cuts there during 1997–2007. Using instrumental variables estimation, they find that the more skill-intensive firms that import better-quality inputs are also the ones that upgrade output quality.

To summarise, whether tariff reductions upgrade or downgrade quality depends on the nature of the export good, that is, on the relative skill intensity of its higher-quality varieties. Moreover, when quality-differentiated export goods of a developing country differ from each other in terms of the relative skill intensity of their respective higher-quality varieties, tariff reduction on imported consumption goods does not uniformly affect the quality of such goods. Reduction of input tariffs also affects the quality of different types of export good asymmetrically, depending on the intensity of the imported inputs relative to the domestic inputs. All these provide plausible explanations of the asymmetric quality variations across different export products that we observed earlier for quite a few developing countries.

4.2 Exchange Rate Policies

Another standard trade policy usually adopted by developing countries with the aim of making exports to the rich world cheaper is exchange rate policy. This takes the form of currency devaluation in countries under a pegged regime – for example, most of the oil-exporting countries in the Middle East and Asia – and policy interventions to moderate exchange rate appreciations that erode the price competitiveness of exports in countries that have adopted a managed float. The links between exchange rate fluctuations and the corresponding adjustments in export prices and export volumes have been well explored (McKenzie, 1999; Martín and Rodríguez, 2004; Gopinath and Rigobon, 2008; Thorbecke and Simith, 2010; Berman, Martin and Mayer, 2012; Li, Ma and Xu, 2015). However, the implications for quality choice and the consequent gains from trade in a world that values higher quality over cheaper varieties of goods and services remain less investigated.

Among the few existing studies, Yu (2013) theoretically explores how exchange rate pass-through depends on firm heterogeneity in productivity and product differentiation in quality. Extending the model devised byAntoniades (2008), Yu (2013) considers the quantity-dependent component of quality-upgrading cost in addition to the quantity-invariant R&D cost of quality upgrading. This allows an exporting firm to choose different quality levels for different markets in order to absorb the exchange rate changes, in addition to adjusting its mark-ups given the linear demand structure. While this analysis sheds some light on the link between exchange rate fluctuations and quality of export goods, it does not decompose domestic factor costs into skill and capital components that may or may not move in tandem as a consequence of inter-sectoral reallocations of these resources following exchange rate shocks. Hu et al. (2014), on the other hand, highlight the impact of exchange rates on firm-level imported intermediates and argue that a decrease in firm-level import exchange rate (i.e. an appreciation in the domestic currency) enables firms to buy higher-quality intermediates, which they could not have afforded before. Hu et al. (2014) verify their theoretical model's predictions using a rich and unique database of Chinese firms' trade data. Chen and Juvenal (2014) show that the elasticity of demand perceived by exporters decreases with both real depreciation and quality. In response to real depreciation, firms significantly increase more of their mark-ups and less of their export volumes for higher-quality products. Given that higher-income countries have a stronger preference for higher-quality goods, this heterogeneous response of prices and quantities to exchange rate changes is predicted to be stronger for exports to high-income destination countries. The predictions are empirically tested using disaggregated Argentinean firm-level wine export values and volumes between 2002 and 2009, with experts' wine ratings as a measure of quality. More recently, Chen, Lu and Tian (2021) establish that credit-constrained firms may upgrade their export product quality in response to foreign currency appreciation. However, they consider labour to be the only factor of production and do not distinguish between different types of export good in terms of their factor (domestic as well as imported) intensities and product quality. In contrast, the theoretical analysis of Ganguly and Acharyya (2022b) shows that, though currency devaluation may raise revenue from exports and thus incentivise quality choice, quality upgrading is still not a foregone conclusion because it also raises the cost of the imported and domestic inputs necessary for quality upgrading. Their result can be illustrated in the extended A–J framework with a rigid unskilled money wage throughout the economy. Assuming e to be the officially pegged exchange rate – units of domestic currency per unit of foreign currency (say, US dollar) – the price-average cost conditions in the (T, N) nugget should now be rewritten as:

$$P_T = eP_T^W = a_{LT}\overline{w} + a_{KT}r + a_{IT}(1 + \tau)eP_I^W \tag{36}$$

$$P_N = a_{LN}\overline{w} + a_{KN}r \tag{37}$$

Due to money wage rigidity, the rate of return to capital is solely and uniquely determined by the nominal exchange rate, given the state of technology, the imported input tariff rate and the world prices of T and I. This, in turn, determines the skilled wage for any given level of export quality from the zero-profit condition (refer back to Equation (26)). So the factor prices are delinked and independent from quality and output changes, and are determined solely by policy for any given state of technology, price of the composite traded good and price of the imported input. Note that the price of non-traded goods is now cost determined.

In this set-up, a devaluation of the domestic currency generates two effects. First, marginal revenue earned from per unit production of good Z rises by the exact rate of currency devaluation at the initial choice of quality and the corresponding world price in foreign currency P_Z^W. At the initial rate of return to capital, this would cause the skilled wage to rise more than proportionately by the magnitude $\frac{\hat{e}}{\theta_{SZ}}$.[29] Second, devaluation also raises the *effective* revenue $(eP_T^W - a_{IT}(1 + \tau)eP_I^W)$ earned by producers of the composite traded good by $(1 - \theta_{IT})\hat{e}$. This will induce producers to raise the level of output of this good, which in turn will entail an increased demand for both unskilled labour and capital. Unskilled labour can be drawn from the existing pool of unemployed workers at the fixed money wage. But, capital being fully employed, the increased demand for capital causes its rate of return to rise by a magnitude even greater than the rate of devaluation, $\frac{(1-\theta_{IT})\hat{e}}{\theta_{KT}}$. For any given domestic-currency price of Z, this in turn lowers the skilled wage by the magnitude $\frac{(1-\theta_{IT})\theta_{KZ}\hat{e}}{\theta_{KT}}$. Thus, the final change in the skilled wage is ambiguous:

$$\hat{w}_S = \left[\frac{1}{\theta_{SZ}} - \frac{(1 - \theta_{IT})\theta_{KZ}}{\theta_{SZ}\theta_{KT}}\right]\hat{e} = \frac{\theta_{KT} - (1 - \theta_{IT})\theta_{KZ}}{\theta_{SZ}\theta_{KT}}\hat{e} \qquad (38)$$

However, even when the skilled wage increases, it increases less than proportionate to the rate of devaluation (i.e. $\hat{w}_S - \hat{e} < 0$). Thus, $\hat{r} > \hat{e} > \hat{w}_S$.

Now, for change in quality, what matters is whether the MC of quality rises more or less than proportionately to the marginal revenue (which is equal to the rate of devaluation) at the initial level of quality. Again, this depends on the relative skill intensity of the higher quality of export good Z. As can be verified algebraically from the marginal condition, quality is upgraded if $\gamma_{SZ} > \gamma_{KZ}$, and downgraded if $\gamma_{SZ} < \gamma_{KZ}$. Note that devaluation raises export quality under the same conditions as reduction of tariff on imported inputs used by the composite traded good raises export quality. This is not surprising because both policies expand the production of composite traded goods: while input tariff reduction raises the effective price received by producers, devaluation raises the price received by them in the domestic currency. In either case, increased production raises the demand for both unskilled labour and capital. At the initial level of quality of the export good Z, the excess demand for capital raises its rate of return. Consequent higher capital cost induces producers of Z to lower their production levels and consequently the demand for skilled workers. The skilled wage thus falls. Therefore, the MC of quality rises – and correspondingly the quality is downgraded – if higher qualities of good Z are relatively capital intensive. Devaluation also raises the price (and the marginal revenue) received by producers of Z in the domestic currency, but it is not a large enough increase to outweigh the increase in the MC and thus induce them to upgrade quality.

---

[29] A hat over a variable denotes its proportional change, e.g. $\hat{e} = \frac{de}{e}$.

Again, for an economy that has a heterogeneous export basket, this result indicates that devaluation will have asymmetric effects on the quality of such products. To illustrate, once again consider the analytical structure of Ganguly and Acharyya (2021) with two types of quality-differentiated export good, as discussed in Section 4.1.1. For export good Z_1, for which $\gamma_{KZ}^1 > \gamma_{SZ}^1$ and which uses the same capital as an import-competing good, devaluation will unambiguously lower its export quality. Note that, without any imported input, and with the import-competing good produced by K_1-type capital and unskilled labour, devaluation raises the rate of return to capital by $\frac{\hat{e}}{\theta_{KY}}$ and, following a similar logic to that spelt out earlier for the extended A–J framework, changes the skilled wage by $\hat{w}_S = \frac{\theta_{KY} - \theta_{KZ}^1}{\theta_{SZ}^1 \theta_{KY}} \hat{e}$. Again, even if the skilled wage rises, it will rise less than proportionate to the rate of devaluation such that $\hat{r}_1 > \hat{e} > \hat{w}_S$. Thus, given $\gamma_{KZ}^1 > \gamma_{SZ}^1$, Q_1 will be downgraded. For the other good, Z_2, for which $\gamma_{KZ}^2 < \gamma_{SZ}^2$ and which is produced by the specific K_2-type capital along with skilled labour, devaluation will improve its quality since $\hat{r}_2 > \hat{e} > \hat{w}_S$ when the skilled wage rises.

These asymmetric effects of devaluation, however, are in sharp contrast with the asymmetric effects of tariff reduction on the import of good Y discussed in Section 4.1.1. The contrasting effect arises because devaluation, unlike tariff reduction, raises the demand for capital and accordingly its rate of return, and correspondingly lowers the skilled wage. The MC of quality thus rises under devaluation for those export goods for which higher quality is relatively more capital intensive, thereby forcing producers of such goods to downgrade quality. These contrasting effects of devaluation and tariff reduction bring out the importance of designing a quality-promoting policy that is specifically tailored to the target group of export products.

4.3 Cross-Country Factor Movements

During the last two decades there has been a surge in emigration of both skilled and unskilled workers, mainly from developing to developed countries. According to the Migration Data Portal, the top three origin countries are India, Mexico and China; up until 2019, these sent out, respectively, 17.5 million, 11.8 million and 10.7 million workers. Despite opening up a source of national income in the form of remittances from these emigrants, such factor outflow directly lowers the productive capacity of the origin economy. Several studies discuss different channels through which emigration of workers may promote exports at the intensive margin. While Rauch and Trindade (2002), Felbermayr and Toubal (2012), Genc et al. (2011) and Ehrhart et al. (2014) give a demand-side explanation through networking,

Rauch and Casella (2003) present the home preference effect. In the context of migration affecting quality of exports (gains at the extensive margin), this networking effect may be relevant in cases such as Akerlof's (1970) lemons problem under asymmetric information of foreign buyers. However, for search goods, i.e. goods with observable quality, the cost effect of emigration might seem more relevant than the demand effect through networking.

It may be obvious that emigration of skilled labour lowers export quality in the native or origin country. A ceteris paribus outflow of skilled labour from developing countries due to higher skilled wages abroad (the pull factor of emigration) pushes up the skilled wage by generating a scarcity. If export quality upgrading requires more intensive use of skilled labour, this will increase the MC of raising quality and thus downgrade export quality. Lower quality goods will lower the MWP of buyers in export destinations, thus further sinking the export prospects of the origin country. This provides an additional dimension to the gains and losses from emigration of skilled workers discussed in the existing literature on brain drain and brain gain. A wide range of arguments have been put forward in such literature from both the origin- and the host-country perspectives (see Commander, Kangasniemi and Winters, 2004, for an earlier survey). Among the benefits that developed host economies get from immigration of skilled workers, easing out of skill shortages resulting from rapid skill-biased technical change is an important one. For developing origin countries, on the other hand, the literature puts forward two important gains. First, emigration of skilled labour may motivate others to acquire more education and technical skills. As long as only a fraction of them emigrate, there may thus be larger human capital available to the origin country, which in turn may promote its growth. Second, emigrants may contribute to investment, capital formation and growth in their native developing countries through networks and remittances (Wei and Balasubramanyam, 2006; Wei et al., 2017). However, while these benefits of emigration of skilled workers may be realised in the long run, in the short run further skill shortages in already skilled-labour-scarce developing countries may cause exporters to downgrade the quality of their products, thereby retarding export growth.

In contrast, emigration of unskilled labour may seem to be not so worrying since it is not directly used in the quality upgrading of skill-based export goods. But trade literature (Jones and Marjit, 1992; Marjit and Beladi, 1999; Acharyya, Beladi and Kar, 2019) often talks about complementarity between wages of different skill types. This implies that emigration of unskilled labour can have adverse implications for export quality upgrading and thus for export prospects through the consequent increase in the skilled wage (Ganguly and Acharyya, 2020).

Consider a variant of the analytical structure discussed in Section 4.1.1, with two changes. First, only the Z_1-type quality-differentiated export good is produced along with homogeneous export good X and import-competing good Y. This is to simplify the analysis. Second, in both X and Y sectors, the unskilled wages are flexible. With these simplifications, suppose α and β are the proportions of skilled and unskilled workers, respectively, who emigrate abroad. The full employment conditions can thus be written as:

$$(1 - \alpha)\overline{S} = a_{SZ}(Q)Z \tag{39}$$

$$(1 - \beta)\overline{L} = a_{LX}X + a_{LY}Y \tag{40}$$

$$\overline{T} = a_{TX}X \tag{41}$$

$$\overline{K} = a_{KZ}(Q)Z + a_{KY}Y \tag{42}$$

The property of this structure that deserves attention is that at any given level of quality, the skilled and unskilled wages are complementary to each other, that is, move in the same direction, whereas the rate of return to capital (and also land) changes in the opposite direction. It follows from here that the unskilled wage and the choice of export quality are interdependent, causing each other. Along with the complementarity between skilled and unskilled wages, we can derive a causality from unskilled wage to export quality as represented by the QQ curve in Figure 9, the nature of which depends again on whether $\gamma_{SZ} > \gamma_{KZ}$ or $\gamma_{SZ} > \gamma_{KZ}$. On the other hand, change in export quality causes a change in the unskilled wage through the change in capital availability for production of the import-competing good and consequent change in the composition of output levels in the (X, Y) nugget. Again, the nature of this causal relationship, represented by the ww curve, depends on γ_{SZ} and γ_{KZ}, but in exactly the opposite way: positively sloped if $\gamma_{SZ} > \gamma_{KZ}$, and negatively sloped otherwise.

Now, an exogenous increase in the emigration rate of unskilled workers raises the unskilled wage due to a consequent fall in unskilled workers' availability for domestic production of homogeneous traded goods, X and Y. By complementarity of wages, this raises the skilled wage and lowers the rates of return to capital and land. Thus, emigration of unskilled workers raises the quality of export good Z if its higher quality is relatively capital intensive, $\gamma_{KZ} > \gamma_{KZ}$, and lowers export quality otherwise, as is evident from the shifts of the ww curve in Figure 9.

If we allow for endogeneity of emigration with the rate of emigration responding to both source-country factors (push factors) and host- or

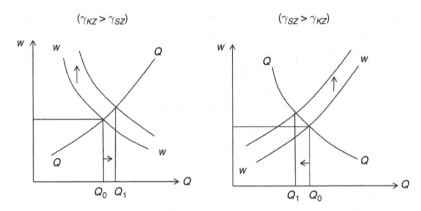

Figure 9 Emigration, export quality and unskilled wage

destination-country factors (pull factors), then quality variations due to any policy or exogenous shock will cause the rate of emigration to change as well. This is evident from the following emigration equilibrium condition:

$$w(\beta, Q) = w^* \tag{43}$$

Note that workers decide to emigrate by equating the gain from migration to its opportunity cost, which is the domestic wages forgone.

Given this interdependence between export quality and rate of emigration, an exogenous shock that triggers larger emigration of unskilled workers at the initial export-quality level will cause quality upgrading by a larger extent and will induce subsequent multiplier expansion in the emigration rate if $\gamma_{KZ} > \gamma_{SZ}$.[30]

To summarise, although unskilled workers are not directly used in the production of quality-differentiated export goods, emigration of such workers may downgrade the quality of export goods. This happens because of the complementarity between emigration of skilled and unskilled workers. Thus, developing countries such as China and India, in particular, from which a significant number of unskilled (as well as skilled) workers emigrate to developed countries, may experience downgrading of the quality of certain of their export good types and, consequently, a dip in earnings from such exports. Moreover, since quality changes also affect the rate of emigration of unskilled workers, an initial shock that triggers emigration of unskilled workers may have a magnified quality-downgrading effect.

---

[30] See Ganguly and Acharyya (2020) for details.

4.4 Direct Export Quality Promotion Subsidies

The discussions in the preceding sections have shown that neither export-promotion policies such as tariff cuts nor exchange rate interventions and increased cross-country factor flows have an across-the-board favourable effect on choice of export quality. That is, whether they induce quality upgrading or downgrading depends on the type of quality-differentiated export product, as the different types vary in terms of the domestic (skill and/or capital) and imported inputs needed to produce their higher-quality varieties. In such situations, targeted subsidies, such as production subsidies linked to quality level and/or input subsidies provided to producers of adversely hit export goods, can be effective solutions. In Sections 4.4.1 and 4.4.2 we discuss such concurrent policies.

4.4.1 Quality–Content Production Subsidy

As discussed in Section 4.1.1, when there are two types of quality-differentiated export good, Z_1 and Z_2, tariff reduction on the final import good worsens the quality of that good (Z_2) whose higher qualities are relatively more skill intensive. Suppose that a per unit production subsidy, $\psi(Q_2)$, the rate of which increases with Q_2, is provided to the producers of good Z_2, such as:[31]

$$\psi(Q_2) = \frac{1}{2} b Q_2^2 \, \forall \, Q_2 \in [0,1] \tag{44}$$

So the zero-profit condition for Z_2 can be rewritten as follows:

$$P_{Z2}^W(Q_2) + \frac{1}{2} b Q_2^2 = a_{KZ}^2(Q_2) r_2 + a_{SZ}^2(Q_2) w_S \tag{45}$$

The subsidy will raise the *effective* marginal revenue for quality, but still may not incentivise quality upgrading as the MC of raising quality will rise as well. To see how, recall that while the two goods Z_1 and Z_2 use two different types of capital, they share the same skilled labour. As the subsidised producers intend to raise quality, they will require more units of both skill and K_2-type capital. While skilled labour can be drawn from the other sector, Z_1, at the given skilled wage, higher demand for sector-specific K_2-type capital will raise its rate of return r_2. So, other than the rise in effective marginal revenue, the capital cost of raising quality Q_2 also rises at the margin, rendering the effect of a quality–content production subsidy uncertain. As explained in Ganguly and Acharyya (2021), at the lower final import tariff rate following a tariff liberalisation

---

[31] It is implicit that a uniform subsidy independent of quality level will not incentivise quality upgrading.

policy, the quality of Z_2 will be upgraded as producers receive a quality–content production subsidy at the rate b, if $\gamma_{KZ}^2 < 2$. To explain briefly, a 1 per cent increase in the rate of subsidy raises the effective marginal revenue from quality upgrading by 1 per cent. On the other hand, since a 1 per cent increase in the rate of return to capital r_2 raises the MC by $\theta_{KZ}^2 \gamma_{KZ}^2$, by the quadratic form of the subsidy function, a 1 per cent rise in the rate of production subsidy raises the MC of quality upgrading by $\frac{\gamma_{KZ}^2}{2}$ per cent. Thus, if $\gamma_{KZ}^2 < 2$, the marginal revenue from quality upgrading is larger than the MC following a 1 per cent increase in the rate of per unit production subsidy, so that producers are incentivised to raise quality.

4.4.2 Input Subsidies

A skilled-wage subsidy provided to the producers of Z_2 can be another effective concurrent policy. Suppose the government offers an ad valorem subsidy at the rate s to producers of Z_2 for skilled wages per unit they pay to skilled workers. So the effective skilled wage that they have to pay to each skilled worker is $\tilde{w}_S = (1 - s)w_S$. This will lower the MC of quality. At the same time, with the wage received by the skilled workers tied down by the lower tariff rate on the import-competing good, as explained earlier, as this wage subsidy encourages producers to expand the scale of production, it raises the demand for K_2-type capital specific to this sector and hence raises its rate of return. Thus, the MC of quality upgrading rises on this account. Overall, however, the MC declines since higher qualities of Z_2 are relatively more skill intensive. Thus, a skilled-wage subsidy mitigates the adverse effect of tariff reduction on the quality of export products, for which higher qualities are relatively skill intensive.

But an input subsidy for use of K_2-type capital, on the other hand, would be ineffective in reversing the adverse effect that tariff reduction has. Just as in the case of the skilled-wage subsidy, the ad valorem subsidy for K_2 will also induce a rise in the rate of return r_2, but now proportionate to the rate of capital subsidy such that the *effective* capital cost per unit does not change, at initial level of quality Q_2. So, with the skilled wage not being affected by the capital subsidy, the MC of raising quality does not change and there will thus be no incentive to upgrade Q_2.

Interestingly, an indirect capital-input subsidy given to the producers of Z_1 (the good that was favourably affected by the tariff cut) might work in favour of Z_2 provided there is flexible coefficient production technology for quality upgrading. Such a capital-input subsidy would raise the skilled wage, given that the rate of return to K_1-type capital used in the production of Z_1 is tied down by the tariff rate. This, in turn, would further downgrade the quality of Z_2 (though it would further upgrade Q_1) under the fixed coefficient production technology, despite a fall in r_2. But under a flexible coefficient production technology, the producers of Z_2 could respond to this rise in wage–rental ratio by substituting skilled labour with K_2-type capital, instead of lowering the quality of Z_2. However, this would happen depending on the extent to which the producers were able to adjust the *additional* requirements of skilled labour and capital for quality upgrading in response to changes in the (effective) factor price ratio. Ganguly and Acharyya (2021) detail out these subsidy policies and also discuss ways of financing such subsidies through government-imposed taxes, such as income taxes on skilled workers and capital owners. Taxing the incomes remitted home by unskilled and/or skilled emigrants can be another way to finance a production subsidy (see Ganguly and Acharyya (2020)).

4.5 Role of Industrial Policy under Asymmetric Information

In Section 3 we discussed how quality being unobserved by consumers and consequent asymmetric information lead to moral hazards and adverse selection problems, and how, accordingly, bad quality drives good quality out of the market (the so-called lemons problem). Since consumers associate the quality of a good they consume with its country of origin, one policy that works in favour of potentially high-quality producers in a country for which consumers have poor country-of-origin perception is having export-quality standards and quality certifications for the products of individual exporting firms.

Quality labelling, like ISO 9000 and ISO 14000 certifications, signals to consumers that the product has attained a minimum quality standard. A potentially high-quality producer in a developing country can thus get a higher price than she would get based on buyers' perceptions of the average industry quality. Developing countries and companies therein increasingly use management and ISO 9000 certifications to overcome reputation problems and signal their investment into quality upgrading and quality performance (Hudson and Jones, 2003; Potoski and Prakash, 2009; Ferro, 2011; Montiel, Husted and Christmann, 2012). Despite the potential advantage of overcoming the negative informational externality problem arising from poor average industry quality, obtaining ISO certificates from certifying bodies is quite costly. Such costs involve not only application and process fees but also organisational restructuring and product standardisation costs, which are often not affordable for small producers in developing countries. In fact, these costs are usually higher in developing countries than in developed countries and can be a barrier to trade (Maskus, Otsuki and Wilson, 2005; Clougherty and Grajek, 2008, 2014; Auriol and Schilizzi, 2015). This necessitates government subsidies, which are also socially optimal since the social marginal benefit of obtaining such certificates and thereby reducing information externality is much higher than the private marginal benefits.

There is, however, contrasting evidence on the effect of ISO certifications. A survey on exporting firms in Bangladesh conducted by Raychaudhuri et al. (2003) reveals that 36 per cent of these firms experienced an increase in their domestic as well as export sales after obtaining ISO 9000 certification. Expectedly, Clougherty and Grajek (2008) find ISO certification to be more beneficial for developing countries than developed countries. However, Hudson and Jones (2003) observe that use of ISO may not fully eliminate informational asymmetry. One reason is that consumers in developed countries often rely more on domestic standards than on ISO 9000 certifications. This is not only because they are more familiar with the domestic standards but also because of the way ISO 9000 accreditation is organised. On the other hand, the study by Dunu and Ayokanmbi (2008) on the impact of ISO 9000 certification on an organisation's financial performance reveals that such certification does not significantly increase the ratio either of revenue to assets or of operating income to assets. Subsequent studies have observed that the beneficial effect of ISO 9000 certification is contingent upon many institutional factors. For example, Sanetra and Marban (2007) and Peuckert (2014) argue that signalling unobserved quality characteristics through ISO certification depends on the credibility of the certifying institutions, which they termed 'quality infrastructure'. On the other hand, Sung and Reinert (2009) identify institutional capacity as the ability of governments and private entities to deliver essential services and develop original measures of four dimensions of standards-related institutional capacity, namely information, conformity, enforcement and international standard-setting. They incorporate these measures into a gravity model to assess their capacity in offsetting the negative effects of standard and technical regulations such as Aflatoxin B1 on food and agricultural product trade. More recently, Blind, Mangelsdorf and Pohlisch (2018, p. 50) argue that the impact of ISO certification signalling quality upgrading depends on the 'trust in the accreditation system and the development status of a country'. The signalling power of certificates is stronger when certification bodies are recognised by accreditation bodies that are signatories to the Multilateral Recognition Arrangement of the International Accreditation Forum (IAF MLA). Blind et al. (2018) used a gravity model for the period 1999–2012 to show that certification promotes trade and that signatories to the IAF MLA trade significantly more. This result underlies the importance of support for accreditation institutions in developing countries. The reputation of the accreditation bodies increases if they are recognised through the IAF MLA, which in turn strengthens the signalling effects and accordingly boosts trade.

That certification by independent agencies or third parties is an effective way for producers of high-quality products to distinguish themselves from the industry average and disseminate product-quality signals to consumers has been emphasised by some recent studies as well (Van Loo et al., 2011; Janssen and Hamm, 2012; Bruschi et al., 2015; Elfenbein, Fisman and McManus, 2015). Ortega et al. (2011) point out that one of the reliable sources of such information are the results of food-safety sampling tests published by the government. The effect of the government's disclosure of food-quality and food-safety information on the food-quality performance of suppliers is investigated in quite a few studies. For example, evaluating the impact of the hygiene quality grade cards policy in Los Angeles in the USA, Jin and Leslie (2003) find that the hygiene quality of restaurants improved significantly. Similarly, Ollinger and Bovay (2020) observe that both the credible threat and actual actions of public disclosure of chicken quality and safety by the government led to improvement in quality and safety by chicken slaughterers.

The optimal quality certification in terms of the power of certification in motivating producers to improve the quality of their products has, of late, been studied theoretically in a moral hazard setting by Zapechelnyuk (2020). He shows that when a monopolist chooses quality and price of an indivisible good, simple certification systems like quality assurance and pass-fail rules are optimal for the regulator that maximises consumers' surplus.

An interesting dimension of quality certification is online marketplaces with quality certifications/badges for sellers. Online marketplaces often use seller reputation scores and badges to certify that sellers meet some minimum quality threshold. Examples are the 'Top Rated Seller' badges used by eBay and the labels 'Superhost', used by Airbnb, and 'Top Rated', used by Upwork. In terms of a simple asymmetric information model, Hui, Saeedi and Tadelis (2019) show that the average quality of both badged and unbadged sellers increases under more stringent certification. Moreover, certification induces entry by both the highest-quality and the lowest-quality sellers. Using the predictions of their model and studying the differential impact of the policy change across 400 separate subcategories of the eBay marketplace, Hui et al. (2019) observe that, after the policy change, entry increases more in markets where the fraction of badged sellers fell relatively more, and that the average quality of entrants increases significantly. However, using the reputation scores of online sellers to ascertain quality may make consumers trust certification more than their own information set. And, when certification is not a very transparent procedure and its verification is costly, it may lead to herd behaviour among consumers.[32]

Another policy that may be effective is improving the country-of-origin perception itself by raising the average industry quality. As Chiang and Masson (1988) demonstrate, one way to achieve this is by pursuing a policy of industrial consolidation; another is by issuing export licences to only a few firms. These policies essentially internalise the informational externality and encourage exporting firms to upgrade the quality of their products. A very large number of domestic firms with unknown brands lower the average industry quality and adversely impact country-of-origin perception. Chiang and Masson (1988) cite the example of about 1,000 highly competitive cotton spinning and weaving firms in Taiwan exporting their little-known individual brands in international markets under the label 'Made in Taiwan'. Low export quality is often related to such a highly fragmented industrial structure, necessitating industrial consolidation. Similar in spirit, Donnenfeld and Mayer (1987) demonstrate that a voluntary export restraint can also achieve the socially optimum quality. These arguments, however, rest on the implicit assumption that consumers can correctly assess the average industry quality. It is then obvious that allowing only a single firm to operate in the industry will eliminate all informational externality. But this implicit assumption contradicts the basic premise that quality is unobservable. When industrial concentration is achieved at the extreme with only one firm being given the licence for production and export, say, then the assumption that consumers can correctly perceive the average industry quality means that they can observe the quality of the good that this single firm produces.

4.6 Concluding Remarks

From the discussions in this section emerge a few important lessons for policymakers in developing countries targeting export promotion through upgrading the quality of export products. First, any policy, whether trade and exchange rate liberalisation or allowing factor flows, may cause asymmetric variations in the quality of export goods depending on those goods' relative skill intensities for upgrading quality. Second, different policies have contrasting effects on the quality of a particular type of export good because of their asymmetric effects on the capital cost – and, correspondingly, on the skilled-labour cost – of producing higher quality. Accordingly, while pursuing trade policies that promote exports through upgrading their quality, the policymakers of developing countries must take into account the relative skill intensity of the targeted export products.

---

[32] We thank an anonymous referee for pointing out this possibility.

Third, policies must be targeted instead of being the same across the board. In cases where across-the-board effects of policy changes cannot be avoided – such as when across-the-board tariff reductions are undertaken by a developing country under its commitment as a WTO member, or when the domestic currency is devalued – then those policies must be supplemented by targeted subsidies, such as production subsidies linked to quality level being provided to producers of adversely hit export goods. Input subsidies may also work, although this depends on their nature.

Last but not least, in the case of goods with unobservable qualities, quality labelling, like ISO 9000 and ISO 14000 certifications, to overcome information asymmetry and reputation problems may be an effective solution. But this calls for providing subsidies to exporting firms since such certifications involve high application and processing fees, as well as costly organisational restructuring and product standardisation.

5 Quality Variations, Income Redistribution and Employment

Export-led growth has been a major objective for export-promotion policies in developing countries in targeting improvement in the quality of their export goods. But, since high-quality goods are usually capital and/or skilled labour intensive, export-led growth through quality upgrading is expected to redistribute incomes against unskilled workers and thus worsen wage inequality. If unskilled wages are rigid downward across all sectors, then there may also be a fall in the aggregate employment of unskilled workers through a change in the composition of output and consequent reallocation of capital towards skill-based quality-differentiated export goods. For sector-specific downward rigidity of unskilled wages – as in the case of formal–informal segmented labour markets in many developing countries – even though most (or all) of the unskilled workers displaced from the rigid-wage (or formal) sectors may be absorbed in the flexible-wage (or informal) sectors, wage inequality may still worsen.

These not-so-desirable income distribution and/or employment effects of upgrading of export quality to achieve faster (export-led) growth pose a policy conflict for local governments in developing countries.[33] With a significantly large proportion of the unskilled workforce earning subsistence wages in informal jobs in many developing countries, growth led by policy-induced quality upgrading may be difficult to sustain if unskilled workers are worse off due to further falls in their wages in the informal sectors and/or loss of employment in the

---

[33] Alternatively, this highlights a development paradox. Developing countries that are unable to improve the quality of their export goods are more likely to experience a lower rate of export-led growth. This may worsen income inequality to a lesser extent, but it also limits the scope for growth and hence domestic redistribution policies in favour of the unskilled and the poor.

formal sectors as a consequence.[34] These adverse labour market implications of quality-upgrading export-promotion policies become all the more important and limit the scope of such policies in democratic developing countries.[35]

This section highlights these issues. We begin with the implications of quality upgrading for wage inequality. We then address the impact of export-quality upgrading on the aggregate employment of unskilled workers under across-the-board downward rigidity of the unskilled wage.

5.1 Trade Liberalisation, Quality Variations and Wage Inequality

Motivated by the observed rising trends in wage inequality almost universally across the globe since the 1980s, a large literature has developed over the last three decades that identifies different channels through which liberal trade policies may accentuate wage inequality in both developed and developing countries (see, e.g., Davis, 1996; Feenstra and Hanson, 1996; Marjit and Acharyya, 2003, 2009; Xu, 2003; Marjit and Kar, 2005; Zhu and Trefler, 2005; Chakraborty and Sarkar, 2008, 2010; Chaudhuri and Yabuuchi, 2008; Anwar, 2009). However, none of these have accounted for the quality variations of skill-based exports induced by export-promotion policies as a plausible source and cause of the observed rise in wage inequality.

One of the very few analyses demonstrating that quality upgrading of skill-based exports causes wage inequality to worsen is that of Das (2003). In a two-country model he establishes that free trade improves the quality of the traded good through a pro-competitive effect. This in turn raises the skilled wage because higher qualities are more skilled-labour intensive. The relative wage, however, rises in both the trading countries if they are similar with respect to technology and labour endowment. Otherwise, in a North–South context with the North having more skilled labour absolutely as well as relative to the endowment of unskilled labour in the South, the relative wage increases in the North, whereas it may increase or decrease in the South.

Ma and Dei (2009) have also analysed the impact of quality upgrading on wage inequality. But in their theoretical model, where quality improvement

---

[34] Even if unskilled wages rise through export-led growth, thereby improving the absolute positions of unskilled workers, deteriorating relative positions due to rising wage inequality may be a cause of concern since economic agents often value their relative positions more than their absolute positions.

[35] For example, in a fractionalised economy with conflicting interest groups, democratic governments often adopt moderate policies so that more groups benefit from such policies than are hurt by them, thus averting potential social conflict.

requires more intensive uses of both an imported input and skilled labour, a developing country has an absolute cost disadvantage in all feasible quality levels due to its technological inferiority. This assumption rules out the possibility of intra-industry trade in the quality-differentiated good, unlike Flam and Helpman (1987) or Falvey and Kierzkowski (1987). In Ma and Dei (2009), a developing country can produce some low-quality goods only under an ad valorem tariff on imports of quality-differentiated goods. These different qualities that can be produced domestically under a tariff wall, however, cannot be exported and are essentially non-traded. In such a context, Ma and Dei (2009) show that a reduction of the input tariff improves the quality of domestically produced non-traded varieties and worsens wage inequality.

The quality upgrading of differentiated export goods induced by tariff reduction on the imported input used in the production of other export goods can also worsen wage inequality. To exemplify, consider the extended A–J framework. As shown in Section 4, a tariff reduction on an imported input used by a composite traded good raises the effective domestic price of the composite traded good: $\tilde{P}_T^W = P_T^W - a_{IT}(1 + \tau)P_I^W$. *At initial quality of the skill-based export good Z*, this raises the rate of return to capital and lowers the unskilled wage by the standard price-magnification effect since the non-traded good is unskilled labour intensive relative to the composite traded good. Higher capital cost forces producers of good Z to lay off skilled workers and contract production. Competition among skilled workers lowers the skilled wage to the level that allows the producers to break even. Thus, at the initial level of quality of Z, input-tariff reduction lowers both the skilled and the unskilled wages. There will, however, be secondary effects on wages through changes in the quality of Z induced by this tariff reduction. Recall that input-tariff reduction improves quality if higher qualities are relatively skill intensive ($\gamma_{SZ} > \gamma_{KZ}$), and worsens it otherwise. However, regardless of whether quality is upgraded or downgraded, the demand for capital in Z sector will fall. The reason is simple. Suppose that $\gamma_{SZ} > \gamma_{KZ}$ so that input-tariff reduction improves the quality of Z. This raises the demand for capital by γ_{KZ} at the margin. On the other hand, larger demand for skilled labour for the higher quality lowers the output of Z, due to the specificity of skilled labour, by the magnitude γ_{SZ} at the margin. On account of this *scale effect*, the demand for capital falls. Since $\gamma_{SZ} > \gamma_{KZ}$, overall, the demand for capital in this sector falls. In the opposite case, where $\gamma_{SZ} < \gamma_{KZ}$, export quality is downgraded consequent upon input-tariff reduction, which lowers the demand for capital by γ_{KZ} and for skilled labour by γ_{SZ} at the margin. The latter causes a scale *expansion* requiring a larger amount of capital in Z sector. But by $\gamma_{SZ} < \gamma_{KZ}$, this scale effect is now smaller and thus, again, the overall demand for capital in Z sector falls.[36]

Thus, regardless of the nature of the quality variation induced by an input-tariff reduction, capital availability for the (T, N) nugget rises. By the standard output-magnification effect, this raises output of the composite traded good and lowers that of the non-traded good since the former is relatively capital intensive. Consequently, the price of the non-traded good rises to clear the local market, which, in turn, raises the unskilled wage and lowers the rate of return to capital. The skilled wage rises, too, as a consequence. Though these changes do not reverse the initial declines in the wages and the rate of return to capital, the central point is that quality variations – or, more specifically, quality upgrading – raise the unskilled wage, which minimises the deteriorating absolute position of unskilled workers.[37] However, since the skilled wage rises too, it may be worthwhile examining whether wage inequality worsens on account of quality variations or not. Algebraically, overall changes in the two wages decomposed into primary and secondary effects can be worked out as:

$$\hat{w} = \frac{-\theta_{IT}\theta_{KN}\gamma\hat{\tau} + \theta_{KT}\left[\frac{\lambda_{KZ}(\gamma_{SZ}-\gamma_{KZ})}{\varepsilon_N|\lambda|}\right]\hat{Q}}{|\theta|} \tag{46}$$

$$\hat{w}_S = \frac{-\theta_{KZ}\theta_{IT}\theta_{LN}\gamma\hat{\tau} + \theta_{KZ}\theta_{LT}\left[\frac{\lambda_{KZ}(\gamma_{SZ}-\gamma_{KZ})}{\varepsilon_N|\lambda|}\right]\hat{Q}}{\theta_{SZ}|\theta|} \tag{47}$$

where ε_N is the absolute value of the price elasticity of relative demand for the non-traded good; θ_{ij} is the share of the i-th factor in the unit cost of producing the j-th good; λ_{KZ} is the share of capital used in the Z sector; $|\lambda|$ and $|\theta|$ are, respectively, determinants of employment-share and cost-share matrices (for the (T,N) nugget); and $\gamma \equiv \frac{\tau}{1+\tau}$.

The second terms in the numerator of both these expressions capture the effect of quality variations induced by the input-tariff reduction. Subtracting one from the other and using the expression for quality change gives us the change in wage inequality *consequent upon quality variations*:

$$\hat{w}_S - \hat{w} = \frac{\theta_{KZ}\theta_{IT}\theta_{LT}\theta_{SZ}\theta_{LN}\lambda_{KZ}\gamma\alpha}{\delta\Delta\theta_{SZ}\varepsilon_N|\lambda||\theta|}\left[\frac{\theta_{KZ}}{\theta_{SZ}} - \frac{\theta_{KT}}{\theta_{LT}}\right](\gamma_{SZ}-\gamma_{KZ})^2\hat{\tau} \tag{48}$$

---

[36] This interesting result has been established and formally proved in Ganguly and Acharyya (2021) in different contexts.

[37] Unskilled workers lose in real terms as well since, along with the fall in the unskilled money wage, the price of the non-traded good rises, though the initial rise is moderated to some extent by release of capital from the Z sector consequent upon quality variations.

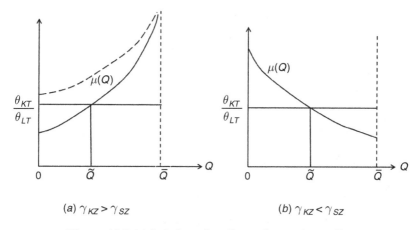

(a) $\gamma_{KZ} > \gamma_{SZ}$ (b) $\gamma_{KZ} < \gamma_{SZ}$

Figure 10 Initial choice of quality and wage inequality

Since, as explained earlier, $\hat{Q} > 0$ if $\gamma_{SZ} > \gamma_{KZ}$, so quality variations worsen wage inequality ($\hat{w}_S - \hat{w} > 0$) if

$$\frac{\theta_{KZ}}{\theta_{SZ}} > \frac{\theta_{KT}}{\theta_{LT}} \tag{49}$$

Note that, given the technological specifications in Equations (28) and (29), $\frac{\theta_{KZ}}{\theta_{SZ}}$ rises with the quality level if higher-quality varieties are relatively more capital intensive, and falls with the quality level otherwise. More precisely, let $\mu(Q) \equiv \frac{\theta_{KZ}(Q)}{\theta_{SZ}(Q)}$. It is straightforward to check that $\mu'(Q) > 0 \ \forall \ Q \in [0, \overline{Q}]$ if $\gamma_{KZ} > \gamma_{SZ}$, and $\mu'(Q) < 0 \ \forall \ Q \in [0, \overline{Q}]$ otherwise. Figure 10 illustrates these alternative cases.[38] In panel (a), the $\mu(Q)$ curve representing the cost-share ratio on the left-hand side of the inequality in Equation (49) is drawn upward sloping for $\gamma_{KZ} > \gamma_{SZ}$, whereas the horizontal line represents the right-hand-side cost–share ratio of the inequality in Equation (49). If the $\mu(Q)$ curve lies above the horizontal line for the entire feasible range of qualities – as shown by the broken curve in panel (a) – then the condition in Equation (49) is always satisfied and therefore wage inequality worsens following an input-tariff reduction regardless of the initial level of quality. But if the $\mu(Q)$ curve intersects the horizontal line from below – as shown by the solid upward-sloping curve – then the condition in Equation (49) is satisfied and thus wage inequality worsens only when the initial quality of good Z is larger than $\tilde{Q}$. In panel (b) we portray this sub-case of conditional worsening of wage inequality when $\gamma_{KZ} < \gamma_{SZ}$ and thus the $\mu(Q)$ curve is downward sloping. In this case, wage inequality worsens if the

---

[38] From Equations (46) and (47) it can be checked that the unskilled wage falls more than the skilled wage by the direct effect of tariff reduction, causing wage inequality to worsen at the initial quality level if $\frac{\theta_{KZ}}{\theta_{SZ}} > \frac{\theta_{KN}}{\theta_{LN}}$. Since, by assumption, the composite traded good is relatively capital intensive, $\frac{\theta_{KT}}{\theta_{LT}} > \frac{\theta_{KN}}{\theta_{LN}}$, the condition in Equation (49) also implies that wage inequality worsens at the initial quality level.

initial quality of good Z is smaller than $\tilde{Q}$. To sum up, whether wage inequality worsens or not through quality variations induced by input-tariff reduction depends on the initial level of quality and on the nature of the export product captured through its relative skill intensity.

On the other hand, Ganguly and Acharyya (2021) demonstrate how incentivising quality upgrading of a skill-based export good through tariff reduction on an imported final consumption good causes wage inequality to worsen. Recall the analytical structure of a small, open economy producing four goods – two quality-differentiated export goods (Z_1 and Z_2), a homogeneous export good (X) and a homogeneous import-competing good (Y) – discussed in Section 4.1.1. The homogenous export good is produced in the informal sector, such as agricultural products, small-scale textiles and/or leather manufacturing and the like. The sector producing the import-competing good, like manufacturing produced in medium to large-scale business set-ups using unskilled workers employed through formal contracts, is the formal sector. In such a set-up, a ceteris paribus reduction in the tariff rate on the final import good Y will increase foreign competition and force the formal-sector import-competing production to contract. This will release both unskilled workers and K_1-type capital. In addition to this, there will be further displacement of unskilled workers through a change in production technique. As scale contraction releases K_1-type capital, r_1 falls at the initial levels of quality and output of Z_1, which induces producers of Y to substitute unskilled labour with capital per unit of output. As the unskilled workers displaced from the contracting formal sector, by the effects of both scale and technique, move to the informal X sector, competition among them and between them and the incumbent workers there lowers the informal wage. That is, tariff reduction causes the unskilled informal wage to fall through informalisation.[39]

On the other hand, as spelt out in Section 4, the skilled wage will rise unambiguously. Recall, at the initial quality of good Z_1, the lower capital cost induces producers of Z_1 to expand output levels. This raises the demand for skilled labour in Z_1, and correspondingly the skilled wage. Therefore, at the initial quality levels of the two skill-based goods, Z_1 and Z_2, wage inequality rises in three dimensions: between skilled workers and formal unskilled workers (captured through the rise in w_S), between skilled workers and informal unskilled workers (since $\hat{w}_S > 0 > \hat{w}$) and between both informal and formal unskilled workers themselves (captured through the fall in w).

---

[39] Another kind of informalisation due to tariff reduction arises in developing countries when production processes are contracted out by firms in the formal import-competing sector to production units in the informal sectors, in a bid to withstand foreign competition. This may cause quality variations across formal-sector and informal-sector production units due to use of different technologies and capital.

Note that these three dimensions of wage inequality arise because of the segmented markets for unskilled workers, that is, the coexistence of formal and informal labour markets. Destruction of formal jobs in developing countries due to import competition and the informalisation of such economies are discussed in Marjit (2003), Marjit, Kar and Beladi (2007), Brady, Kaya and Gereffi (2011) and Bogliaccini (2013). For example, as observed by Bogliaccini (2013), in the more industrially advanced Latin American countries, formal industrial employment declined significantly as a consequence of trade liberalisation and there being no alternative sources of formal employment to which the laid-off industrial workers could be relocated. This reduced the income of those unskilled workers, who were pushed into survival strategies in the informal sectors.

Wage inequality may worsen further as tariff reduction raises Q_1 and lowers Q_2. As shown by Ganguly and Acharyya (2021), these quality variations increase the capital requirement in the quality-differentiated sectors, thereby causing the formal sector to contract further and the unskilled informal wage to fall even more. To explain, as tariff reduction upgrades quality Q_1, it requires more K_1-type capital per unit of output of Z_1 by the magnitude $\gamma_{KZ}^1 \hat{Q}_1$ at the margin. On the other hand, the higher demand for skilled labour as Q_1 is raised lowers the production of good Z_1 by $\gamma_{SZ}^1 \hat{Q}_1$ at the margin. There will be further change in the capital requirement in Z_1 sector induced by the downgrading of Q_2, too. A lower-quality Q_2 requires less skilled labour as well as less K_2-type capital (which is specific to the Z_2 sector) per unit of output. The latter enables production of good Z_2 to expand, which will require additional skilled labour. But, given the assumption that $\gamma_{KZ}^2 < \gamma_{SZ}^2$, overall demand for skilled labour in Z_2 sector falls. The displaced skilled workers move to Z_1 sector, thereby expanding the production of Z_1. Due to this second-round scale expansion, the demand for K_1-type capital rises. Algebraically, denoting the capital requirement in Z_1 sector by $K_{1Z} = a_{KZ}^1(Q)Z_1$, we can derive the proportional change in it in terms of quality variations:

$$\hat{K}_{1Z} = \lambda_{KZ}^1 \left[(\gamma_{KZ}^1 - \gamma_{SZ}^1)\hat{Q}_1 - \frac{\lambda_{SZ}^2}{\lambda_{SZ}^1}(\gamma_{SZ}^2 - \gamma_{KZ}^2)\hat{Q}_2 \right] > 0 \qquad (50)$$

where λ_{KZ}^1 is the share of good Z_1 in the total use of K_1-type capital and λ_{SZ}^m is the share of good m ($m = 1,2$) in the use of skilled labour.

This increased demand for K_1-type capital will be met by drawing it from the import-competing Y sector, thereby inducing further contraction of the formal import-competing sector. This will release more unskilled workers from there, who will migrate to the informal agricultural sector X, causing a further fall in

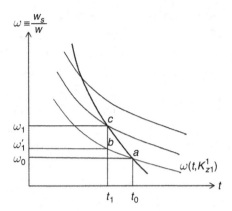

Figure 11 Effect of tariff reduction on wage inequality

the informal unskilled wage. Therefore, quality variations induced by tariff reduction accentuate wage inequality further. This result has important ramifications for the existing literature on trade and wage inequality. Wage inequality worsens to a larger extent when quality variations of skill-based exports are taken into account than when these are not accounted for. Thus, the magnitude of changes in wage inequality due to export-promotion strategies like tariff reduction will be underestimated if quality variations induced by such policies are not accounted for. Figure 11, taken from Ganguly and Acharyya (2021), illustrates this. Each flatter curve indicates the inverse relationship between the skilled–unskilled wage ratio and the tariff rate for any given pair of (Q_1, Q_2) and corresponding level of K_{Z1}^1, whereas a higher curve reflects larger wage inequality corresponding to a larger K_{Z1}^1, for the reasons spelt out earlier. When the tariff is lowered from t_0 to t_1, at initial quality levels wage inequality accentuates from ω_0 to ω_1' (corresponding to movement from point a to point b). Then, it changes further to ω_1 (corresponding to movement from point b to point c on a higher ϖ curve) due to quality variations brought about by the lower tariff. So, taking into account quality variations induced by tariff reduction, the total change in wage inequality should be measured by the movement along the steeper curve.

Note that if the informal agricultural sector had used the same capital K_1 as used in the (Y, Z_1) subsystem, tariff reduction would have had the same asymmetric quality effect. But now the informal wage would rise unambiguously despite a tariff reduction causing informalisation, and so the initial or pre-reform quality of export good Z_1 would matter for whether wage inequality worsened or not.

5.2 Devaluation, Quality Variations and Wage Inequality

Currency devaluation has an altogether different implication for wage inequality, which again suggests that not all types of indirect export-promotion policy have the same or similar effects. To see this, consider the benchmark set-up discussed earlier, taken from Ganguly and Acharyya (2021), with specific factors (land and capital) used in production in the formal and informal sectors. Devaluation of the domestic currency vis-à-vis the foreign currency generates the following general equilibrium effects.

First, this makes imports dearer in domestic currency terms, causing demand for locally produced import-competing goods to rise. The formal-sector production thus expands. This raises demand for both unskilled labour and K_I-type capital, as well as raising the unskilled wage and the rate of return to the K_I-type capital. Note that the informal unskilled wage rises on two counts. One is due to the increasing marginal productivity as unskilled workers are drawn from the informal sector to meet the increased demand in the expanding formal sector. The other is due to there being factor substitution in the formal sector of capital by unskilled labour in the face of higher r_I and fixed formal wage. So, at initial quality levels, devaluation unambiguously raises the informal wage through reduced informalisation. In the case of the skilled wage (see Section 4.2), it may fall or rise depending on whether devaluation raises the marginal revenue from quality less or more than the capital (at the margin) cost of raising quality. Algebraically, the change in skilled wage is given as:

$$\hat{w}_S = \frac{\theta_{KY} - \theta_{KZ}^1}{\theta_{SZ}^1 \theta_{KY}} \hat{e} \tag{51}$$

Thus, $\hat{w}_S > 0$ if $\theta_{KY} > \theta_{KZ}^1$. At the initial quality levels, however, wage inequality may decline even if the skilled wage increases. Quality changes induced by currency devaluation will bring in further changes in the informal unskilled wage and, correspondingly, wage inequality. Recall from Section 4 that currency devaluation lowers Q_1 and raises Q_2 and thus by Equation (50) $K_{Z1}^1 < 0$. That is, devaluation-induced quality variations release some K_I-type capital, which allows the formal sector to expand. The informalisation falls, further raising the unskilled informal wage. So, quality variations now lower wage inequality in sharp contrast to what we observed under the tariff reduction discussed earlier. Therefore, even if wage inequality is worsened by devaluation at initial quality levels, it may decline at the new equilibrium.

5.3 Uniform Minimum Wage Laws, Quality Variations and Unemployment

Suppose a uniform minimum wage law is implemented in all sectors. That is, there is no informal or organised sector where competition may drive down unskilled wages even below the minimum wage applied in the formal sectors. If such an across-the-board uniform minimum wage is set above the labour market clearing wage, there will emerge an overall unemployment in the economy.[40] In such a context, the issue at hand is whether quality variations will worsen the unemployment situation or not.

In the extended A–J framework, with the wage to unskilled labour pegged at the level $\bar{w}$ by the government in both the composite traded good and the non-traded good, it can be shown that policy-induced quality variations will unambiguously raise aggregate employment. But the overall employment effect depends on the nature of the policy. At the initial quality level, whereas an input-tariff reduction lowers aggregate employment, a devaluation raises it. To check, first of all, recall from Section 4 that under a rigid unskilled wage, a reduction in the input tariff and a devaluation both raise the rate of return to capital, though by different magnitudes. The corresponding increase in the capital cost raises the price of the non-traded good. Demand for and output of the non-traded good thus falls. On this account, some unskilled workers are laid off. Some capital is also released that enables output of the composite traded good to expand, thereby absorbing some of the unemployed unskilled workers. But this good being relatively capital intensive, fewer workers are absorbed than are laid off. Therefore, aggregate employment falls *at the initial quality level*.[41] On the other hand, for the same reason as discussed earlier, input-tariff-reduction-induced quality variation, regardless of its direction, lowers the demand for capital in the Z sector. Larger availability of capital as a consequence raises the output levels of both the composite traded good and the non-traded good (though at different proportions) and thereby raises the aggregate employment of unskilled workers. Overall, the effect of an input-tariff reduction on the aggregate employment is ambiguous. Since the initial adverse effect is driven by a rise in price of the non-traded good and the consequent fall in its demand and output, its magnitude is larger the larger is the price elasticity of (relative) demand for the non-traded good. Accordingly, taking into account any subsequent increase in the employment level due to quality variation, the aggregate employment increases at the

---

[40] This is typically the case in most of the developing countries since the large pool of unskilled workers potentially makes the market-clearing wage precariously low.

[41] Note that, due to homothetic taste, real income gains from input-tariff reduction do not impact demand for non-traded goods and, accordingly, aggregate employment.

new equilibrium if the price elasticity is sufficiently low. The algebraic details are avoided here, but the precise condition or critical value of the price elasticity of (relative) demand for the non-traded good can be easily worked out.

Currency devaluation, on the other hand, also raises the domestic currency price of the composite traded good net of the domestic currency price of the imported input, the *effective* price, and, by competitive conditions, such a rise must be equal to the increased capital cost. Thus, now the relative price of the non-traded good does not rise unambiguously. More precisely, recalling from Section 4 the magnitude of the proportional rise in the rate of return to capital, $\hat{r} = \frac{1-\theta_{IT}}{\theta_{KT}} \hat{e}$, the proportional change in the relative price of the non-traded good is given by:

$$\hat{P}_N - \hat{P}_T = \left[\frac{(1 - \theta_{IT})\theta_{KN}}{\theta_{KT}} - 1 \right] \hat{e} = \left[\frac{(1 - \theta_{IT})\theta_{KN} - \theta_{KT}}{\theta_{KT}} \right] \hat{e} \qquad (52)$$

So, the relative price of the non-traded good falls under the assumption that it is relatively labour intensive (that is, $\theta_{KN} < \theta_{KT}$). Its demand and output thus rise, drawing labour from the unemployed pool and capital from the composite traded sector, necessitating a fall in output of the composite traded good. A fall in employment due to such contraction, however, is less than the additional workers employed in the non-traded sector. Thus, at the initial quality level, currency devaluation raises aggregate employment, unlike input-tariff reduction. Subsequently, quality variations due to currency devaluation will raise aggregate employment for the same reason as spelt out earlier. Thus, the initial employment increase is reinforced by subsequent quality variations.[42]

5.4 Concluding Remarks

While improving export quality and consequent export earnings through indirect export-promotion strategies is a matter of concern for policymakers in developing countries, the adverse consequences of such quality improvement for the domestic unskilled labour markets cannot be overlooked. However, whether such a policy conflict will arise or not is conditional on several factors. For example, when quality variation is induced by an input-tariff reduction, whether the wage inequality worsens or not depends on the initial level of quality and on the nature of the export product captured through its relative skill intensity. Incentivising quality upgrading of a skill-based export good through reduction of tariff on an imported final consumption good, on the other hand,

---

[42] When no imported input is used in domestic production, Ganguly and Acharyya (2022b) have demonstrated that aggregate employment increases even when non-traded goods are relatively capital intensive ($\theta_{KN} < \theta_{KT}$).

causes wage inequality to worsen unambiguously. By displacing unskilled workers from the contracting formal sector and causing the unskilled informal wage to fall through informalisation, it worsens wage inequality in all three dimensions. Moreover, wage inequality will worsen to a greater extent when quality variations induced by tariff reductions are taken into account. Currency devaluation, however, will have an altogether different implication for wage inequality, which again suggests that not all types of indirect export-promotion policy have the same or similar effects. On the other hand, in economies with prevalence of unemployment of unskilled workers because of implementation of the (uniform) minimum wage laws in all sectors, policy-induced quality variations unambiguously raise the aggregate employment. Still, policy choice may matter because different policies impact aggregate employment in a contrasting manner at the initial quality level. For example, at the initial quality level, whereas an input-tariff reduction lowers aggregate employment, a currency devaluation raises it.

6 Domestic Demand, Market Imperfection and Urban Unemployment

In Sections 4 and 5, we discussed how trade and exchange rate policies affect the quality of export goods, and the implications of such quality variations for wage inequality and aggregate employment of unskilled workers in alternative variants of the competitive general equilibrium structure of a small, open economy. Three assumptions, in particular, made in such contexts may not be good approximations of a typical developing economy. First, it was assumed that the quality-differentiated export goods are not domestically consumed, which certainly is not the case. Second, it was assumed that these goods are produced by competitive firms. This, though not at odds with what we can observe in many developing countries, is certainly not the only type of market structure for domestic production of export goods observed there. Third, as observed by Fields (1990), Marcouiller and Young (1995), Swinnerton (1996) and Rogers and Swinnerton (2004), not all unskilled workers displaced from the formal sectors may be absorbed in the short run in the informal sectors. Thus, some unemployment may still persist, which would add another dimension to the wage inequality among unskilled workers. One way to capture this unemployment dimension is to employ the Harris–Todaro migration condition for labour movement between formal and informal sectors. In this section, we re-examine some of the issues discussed in the previous sections by relaxing these three apparently over-simplifying assumptions regarding the analytical structure of a developing economy.

6.1 Domestic Consumption of Quality-Differentiated Export Goods

To keep things simple, consider the case of only one quality-differentiated good, say, Z_I – and correspondingly only one type of capital in our economy (K_I) – along with the two homogeneous traded goods X and Y. Suppose only skilled workers consume Z_I along with X and Y. Others consume only X and Y. Let $b_Z(Q)$ be the fraction of skilled wage income, $w_S \overline{S}$, that is spent on Z_I, where $b'_Z(Q) > 0$ for all $Q \in [0, 1]$ but $b_Z(1) = \overline{b}_Z < 1$.

From the marginal condition for choice of quality of Z_I, reproduced below from Section 4, it is evident that Q_I will be affected by the spending on consumption of Z_I by the skilled workers only if the skilled wage and the rate of return to capital are affected:

$$P_{Z1}^{W'}(Q_1^0) = a_{KZ}^{m'}(Q_1^0)r_1 + a_{SZ}^{m'}(Q_1^0)w_S \tag{53}$$

But, as is evident from the relevant zero-profit condition, given the rigid unskilled wage in the import-competing sector, the rate of return to capital is tied down by the tariff-inclusive price of imports of Y. This, in turn, ties down the skilled wage for any given Q_I. Moreover, by the envelope theorem, skilled wage remains invariant with respect to changes in the quality level of Z_I. On the other hand, by the small country assumption, a fraction of skilled-wage income now spent on the quality-differentiated export good will only lower the *volume* of exports of Z_I without affecting its world price. Further, as long as the rest of the goods are all traded, there will be no changes in the production levels, either. The output levels of the homogeneous traded goods X and Y will not be constrained by local demand and thus will always be at full employment. Hence, the informal unskilled wage will be invariant with the domestic consumption spending on the quality-differentiated export good and correspondingly smaller spending on X and Y. The only change would be the volume of trade. With less of a fraction of income now being spent on good Y (and on X), demand for Y and thus for imports falls, whereas the volume of agricultural exports rises.[43] But these changes in trade volumes will be inconsequential for the world prices of X and Y as long as the country under consideration is small in the world market. Thus, with world prices of all goods – Z_I, X and Y – remaining unchanged, the skilled wage, the rate of return to capital and the unskilled wage all remain unchanged. This no-impact result implies two things. First, the domestic producers of good Z_I will choose the same level of quality now as when it is not domestically consumed. Second, there will be no change in informalisation and wage inequality.

---

[43] Note that a fall in the volume of exports of Z_I and a corresponding fall in the export value would maintain balanced trade.

By similar reasoning, trade and exchange rate policies will have the same effects as we discussed earlier without any domestic consumption of Z_1. Further, whether only skilled workers or all income earners consume quality-differentiated export goods along with the homogeneous traded good does not matter. The results remain unchanged as long as all goods are traded and the economy under consideration is small in the world market.

Domestic consumption matters, however, when the economy produces some non-traded goods. In such a case, production levels and, consequently, factor prices are no longer independent of the local demand conditions, even for a small, open economy. Consider, for example, the A–J framework in which the small, open economy produces a homogeneous non-traded good (N) along with a homogeneous composite traded good (T) and the quality-differentiated export good (Z). Now, domestic consumption of Z means that smaller fractions of income are spent on the composite traded good and, most importantly, on the non-traded good. For any price level, the demand for the non-traded good falls. The consequent excess supply lowers its price, which in turn lowers the unskilled wage and raises the rate of return to capital by the price-magnification effect as long as the non-traded good is unskilled labour intensive relative to the composite traded good. The skilled wage, on the other hand, falls for reasons spelt out earlier. Thus, by the marginal condition for quality, the quality of the export good Z will rise if higher qualities are more skill and labour intensive ($\gamma_{SZ} > \gamma_{KZ}$). Wage inequality will also change as a consequence of domestic consumption, but its direction will be ambiguous since both the unskilled and the skilled wages decline.

On the other hand, if there are uniform rigid wages causing aggregate unemployment of unskilled workers, then, though domestic consumption of Z will leave its quality unchanged, the aggregate employment will fall unambiguously. Note that, similar to what has been discussed already, with the unskilled wage being rigid, the rate of return to capital is tied down by the world price of the composite traded good and this, in turn, ties down the skilled wage for any given Q_1. With the quality of Z thus remaining unchanged, its output remains the same as well. Hence, there will be no change in the demand for capital in that sector or, correspondingly, in the capital available for the (T, N) nugget, leaving the output levels of the traded and the non-traded goods unchanged. But, since the domestic consumers now spend less on the non-traded (as well as the composite traded) good, so its demand and consequently its output will fall. Released capital on account of this will enable the composite traded good sector to expand. That is, there will be a change in composition of output in the (T, N) nugget away from the non-traded good, causing a fall in the aggregate employment of unskilled labour if it is relatively unskilled labour intensive. The essence of this employment effect of domestic consumption of the quality-differentiated export good Z is similar to a fall in the real income of consumers: it is as if we tax away the part of domestic consumers' income that they spend on T and N.

6.2 Monopoly Production

Suppose Z_1 is produced by a single firm, whereas Z_2 is produced by perfectly competitive firms. As a further simplification, suppose the domestic firm charges a fixed mark-up ϕ over the average factor cost for any given Q_1, which she raises, however, with the quality level: $\phi(Q_1)$, $\phi' > 0$. Since the domestic economy is small in the world market, the market power of this domestic firm is restricted only within the domestic economy. So for any quality level Q_1 that she chooses, the monopolist cannot charge a price higher than $P_{Z1}^W(Q_1)$, such that

$$P_{Z1}^W(Q_1) = \Phi(Q_1).C_{Z1}(Q_1) = \Phi(Q_1)[a_{SZ}^1(Q_1)w_S + a_{KZ}^1(Q_1)r_1] \tag{54}$$

where $\Phi(Q_1) = 1 + \phi(Q_1) > 1$.

For any given mark-up and choice of Q_1, the domestic firm pays a wage to the skilled workers according to Equation (54). Of course, she pays less if she raises her mark-up and vice versa. The quality is chosen by the following marginal condition:

$$\frac{d\pi_{Z1}}{dQ_1} = P_{Z1}^{W\,'}(Q_1) - C_{Z1}(Q_1).\Phi'(Q_1) - \Phi(Q_1).C_{Z1}{}'(Q_1) = 0 \tag{55}$$

First, it can be easily verified that the monopolist will provide a lower quality for any given skilled wage and rate of return to capital, which follows from

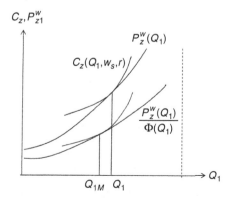

Figure 12 Under-provision of quality by a domestic monopolist

evaluating Equation (55) at Q_I produced by the competitive producers that satisfy the marginal condition in Equation (53):

$$\frac{d\pi_{Z1}}{dQ_1}\bigg|_{Q_1^0} = [1 - \Phi(Q_1^0)]P_{Z1}^{W'}(Q_1^0) - C_{Z1}(Q_1^0).\Phi'(Q_1^0) < 0 \qquad (56)$$

This under-provision of quality result, illustrated in Figure 12, is similar to that established in the partial equilibrium quality choice models discussed in Section 3. The upward-sloping convex curve labelled $P_{Z1}^{W}(Q_1)$ represents the MWP of consumers in the world market, which increases with the quality level of the export good Z_I at the increasing rate. On the other hand, the upward-sloping convex curve labelled $C_{Z1}(Q_1, w_S, r_1)$ represents the unit cost of producing good Z_I, which, by the cost-specifications in Section 3, increases at an increasing rate with the quality level Q_I for any given w_S and r_I. Competitive firms choose quality level Q_I^C corresponding to the tangency between these two curves, so that both the zero-profit condition and the marginal condition are satisfied. The monopolist producer's profit-maximising quality choice is shown by the tangency between a lower unit cost curve – since it pays lower wages to the skilled workers – and the curve labelled $\frac{P_{Z1}^{W}(Q_1)}{\Phi(Q_1)}$, satisfying the conditions in Equations (54) and (55). Note that the vertical distance between the $P_{Z1}^{W}(Q_1)$ and $\frac{P_{Z1}^{W}(Q_1)}{\Phi(Q_1)}$ curves represents the mark-up or profit per unit of output for the monopolist.

Two comments are warranted at this point. First, recall that, given the rate of return to capital, by the envelope theorem, the skilled wage is invariant with respect to quality variations. Thus, the quality of the other type of export good, Z_2, will be the same even though the monopolist provides a lower quality of Z_I.[44] Second, under-provision of quality of Z_I by a domestic monopolist will lower wage inequality. Recall from the discussion in Section 5 and, in particular, Equation (50) that the requirement of (K_I-type) capital in the Z_I sector will fall due to the under-provision of its quality, and there will be no change in the quality of Z_2. The consequent larger availability of capital will cause the formal sector to expand, thereby raising the demand for unskilled labour and the informal unskilled wage.

---

[44] There is a large (partial equilibrium) literature on quality choices under oligopolistic market structures that establish quality differentiation through competition among oligopolistic firms. However, in our general equilibrium analysis with a homogeneous set of consumers having the same MWP for quality, such a possibility of quality differentiation is ruled out; accordingly, such market structures do not add any flavour to our analysis. On the other hand, price or quantity competition among oligopolistic firms results in lower profit mark-up for each of them such that we can expect them to provide a better (uniform) quality than the monopolist. But, the under-provision of quality result still holds as long as the firms can charge a positive (or non-zero) profit mark-up over costs.

Therefore, wage inequality between the skilled workers and the informal unskilled workers, as well as among the unskilled workers themselves, will decline.

6.3 Open Unemployment in the Formal Sector

Despite the existence of informal sectors in developing countries, some workers may remain unemployed. For example, workers aiming at getting a higher wage (and a secure job) in the formal sector, but not being absorbed there at present, may prefer to wait for things to turn better for them in the future. Similarly, some unskilled workers displaced from the formal sector due to a policy shock may prefer to stay back, instead of migrating to agricultural and other informal sectors and taking up informal jobs there, if they expect the job losses in the formal sector(s) to be temporary. These cases are not at odds with developing country experiences since the observed unemployment includes disguised and seasonal unemployment as well as under-employment. One way to capture the prevalence of unemployment despite the existence of informal sectors is to incorporate the following Harris–Todaro migration condition into the analytical framework of Ganguly and Acharyya (2021), defined by the equation system (Equations (30)–(33)) in Section 4:

$$\left[\frac{a_{LY}Y}{\overline{L} - a_{LX}X} \right] \overline{w} = w \tag{57}$$

The term in the brackets on the left-hand side of Equation (57) reflects the probability of getting a job in the formal sector: $a_{LY}Y$ is the number of jobs in the formal sector Y; $a_{LX}X$ is the number of workers engaged in production of X in the informal sector; thus $\overline{L} - a_{LY}Y$ is the number of workers seeking jobs in the formal sector Y. So, the migration equilibrium condition states that the unskilled workers migrate to and/or stay back in the formal sector until the expected unskilled wage there equals the unskilled wage in the informal sector. The aggregate employment is thus less than the total unskilled work-force and is determined by the scale and technique of production in the formal and informal sectors:

$$\overline{L} > L_e = a_{LX}X + a_{LY}Y \tag{58}$$

Now consider a reduction in the ad valorem tariff on imports of Y. It is straightforward to check that its effect on the quality levels of the two differentiated export goods, Z_1 and Z_2, will be the same as discussed in Section 4. Tariff reduction lowers the rate of return to both types of capital and raises the skilled wage. Since, by assumption $\gamma^1_{KZ} > \gamma^1_{SZ}$ and $\gamma^2_{KZ} < \gamma^2_{SZ}$, Q_1 rises and Q_2 falls as a consequence. The informal unskilled wage, on the other hand, declines, as before, through larger informalisation. The formal sector contracts and some unskilled workers are laid off as a consequence of tariff reduction. As the number of jobs contracts in the formal sector, the probability of getting a formal-sector job and, correspondingly, the expected wage there decline, inducing some of the laid-off unskilled workers to migrate to the informal agricultural sector X. Competition for informal jobs lowers the informal unskilled wage as a consequence. Therefore, wage inequality is accentuated in all three of the dimensions discussed earlier.

A rise or fall in aggregate employment, however, depends on the extent to which the informal sector can expand. Since the agricultural good is produced by a specific factor, land, its scale of production is constrained by the technique of production. This is evident from the full employment condition for land (denoted by J): $\bar{J} = a_{JX}X$. The percentage change in the output of X (and the corresponding increase in informal employment) is thus given by $\hat{X} = -\hat{a}_{JX}$. The fall in the unskilled wage, as spelt out above, will induce producers to use more labour-intensive techniques and lower the use of land per unit of output, thereby making it an excess at the initial level of output. This enables a scale expansion; the larger the value of the factor substitution elasticity, the larger the extent of the scale expansion. Since more unskilled workers are employed for the scale expansion, a sufficiently high value of factor substitution elasticity raises the overall employment of unskilled workers by inducing more workers than are laid off in the formal sector to migrate to the informal sector.

To sum up, a reduction of the tariff on final imports has the same asymmetric effect on the quality of differentiated export goods, as discussed earlier. Wage inequality is also accentuated. But aggregate employment may fall if the value of the factor substitution elasticity in the informal sector is not sufficiently large, in which case some of the unskilled workers who have been laid off from the formal sector are worse off. The effects of other policies that were discussed in Section 4 can be similarly analysed.

7 Concluding Remarks

For developing countries, even those such as Brazil, China, India and Mexico that have well-diversified export baskets, the low quality of their exports has been constraining their export growth in the developed country markets, since buyers there are more quality-conscious. This has weakened the export-led growth prospects for developing countries. After documenting the low-export-quality phenomenon, we have discussed several plausible underlying causes of it. While fundamentals like technology and scarcity of skilled labour and capital are important constraints, trade and exchange rate policies can also provide incentives and disincentives for exporting firms when making quality choices. This suggests that there is scope for policymakers to improve the quality of exports and thereby boost exports to strengthen export-led growth for developing countries. When quality upgrading requires better-quality imported inputs, having input-tariff reductions that improve export quality is an obvious way to go. But even when quality upgrading requires intensive use of domestic inputs such as physical capital and skilled labour, reduction of tariffs on either imported inputs or imported final goods can incentivise exporters to upgrade the quality of their products if it changes the prices of such factors in a way that lowers the MC of higher qualities.

Two policy implications follow from the discussions. First, not all policies may have similar effects. Whereas reduction of tariffs on final imported goods may raise the quality of certain types of export product, a policy intervention to prevent the domestic currency appreciating vis-à-vis the foreign currencies may have just the opposite effect. Second, a policy may have an asymmetric effect on different product groups that vary from each other with respect to the skill intensity required for quality upgrading. As discussed in Section 4, a tariff reduction upgrades the quality of an export good that requires larger capital relative to skilled labour for quality upgrading, but downgrades the quality of an export good that requires larger skilled labour relative to capital for quality upgrading. Aerospace products, scientific instruments, defence equipment, household and office equipment, electrical appliances and agro-based products are typical examples of the former type of quality-differentiated export good; software, jewellery, diamond cutting and polishing, IT-enabled services, financial services and the like exemplify the latter type of goods and services.

The low-export-quality phenomenon in developing countries arises largely due to unequal distribution of income, whether it is from the demand side – income disparities among consumers – or from the supply side – domestic factor prices and the consequent factor income distribution. In fact, the policies impact quality choices primarily through affecting factor prices and redistributing factor incomes. A major point highlighted in the present Element is this supply-side analysis of the implications of (factor) income distribution for the quality of exports and of the role of trade, exchange rate and subsidy policies.

Our focus on supply-side links also brings out the two-way causation: export quality and income distribution affect each other. Higher-quality varieties are usually intensive in terms of domestic factors like skilled labour and/or capital, but not so much in terms of unskilled labour. Thus, it may be that higher quality induced by direct or indirect export-promotion policy measures raises the relative demand for these factors and worsens the relative position of unskilled workers by redistributing incomes away from them, thereby accentuating (income) inequalities. In cases of labour market inflexibility, such as institutionally given wage rates, prevalent in many least developed countries, on the other hand, quality upgrading may be accompanied by a fall in the aggregate employment of unskilled workers. This indicates a conflict of policy targets: a trade-off between higher export quality and greater aggregate employment. These issues – the reverse causality from export quality to income (or wage) inequality and employment – not only are important in themselves but also have, in many instances, conditioned the continuation or reversal of liberal trade and export-promotion policies. Though it has not been explored in this Element, in the case of income disparities among buyers resulting in low quality of export goods, a redistribution of incomes can also improve export quality. In fact, since, in a general equilibrium setting, unequal distribution of endowment of resources and factors of production among individuals and households results in unequal distribution of income among them, so trade and exchange rate policies can have a demand-side effect as well, through redistribution of factor incomes.

Bibliography

AbdGhani, N. H., NikMat, N. K. & Sulaiman, Y. (2019). Export performance: The role of product quality and market orientation. *WSEAS Transactions on Business and Economics*, **16**(25), 215–25.

Acharyya, R. (1998). Monopoly and product quality: Separating or pooling menu? *Economics Letters*, **61**(2), 187–94.

Acharyya, R. (2005). *Product Standards, Employment and Exports: An Analytical Study*. Heidelberg: Physica/Springer Verlag.

Acharyya, R. & Jones, R. W. (2001). Export quality and income distribution in a small dependent economy. *International Review of Economics and Finance,* **10**, 337–51.

Acharyya, R., Beladi, H. & Kar, S. (2019). Trade, migration costs and asymmetric migration patterns. *World Economy*, **42**, 2629–48.

Akerlof, G. A. (1970). The market for 'lemons': Quality uncertainty and the market mechanism. *Quarterly Journal of Economics*, **84**(3), 488–500.

Allen, F. (1984). Reputation and product quality. *RAND Journal of Economics*, **15**(3), 311–27.

Amiti, M. & Khandelwal, A. K. (2009). *Import Competition and Quality Upgrading*. NBER Working Paper 15503. Cambridge, MA: National Bureau of Economic Research. www.nber.org/papers/w15503.

Antoniades, A. (2008). Heterogeneous firms, quality, and trade. *Journal of International Economics,* **95**(2), 263–73.

Anwar, S. (2009). Wage inequality, welfare and downsizing. *Economics Letters,* **103**, 75–7.

Auriol, E. & Schilizzi, S. G. (2015). Quality signalling through certification in developing countries. *Journal of Development Economics,* **116**, 105–21.

Bas, M. & Paunov, C. (2021). Input quality and skills are complementary and increase output quality: Causal evidence from Ecuador's trade liberalization. *Journal of Development Economics*, **151**(C). DOI: https://doi.org/10.1016/j.jdeveco.2021.102668.

Bas, M. & Strauss-Khan, V. (2013). Input-trade liberalization, export prices and quality upgrading. *Journal of International Economics*, **95**(2), 250–62.

Bayudan-Dacuycuy, C. & Lim, J. A. (2014). Chronic and transient poverty and vulnerability to poverty in the Philippines: Evidence using a simple spells approach. *Social Indicators Research*, **118**(1), 389–413.

Benkovskis, K. & Wörz, J. (2012). *Non-price Competitiveness of Exports from Emerging Countries*. FIW Working Paper 100. Vienna: FIW – Research

Centre International Economics, Vienna. www.econstor.eu/bitstream/10419/121110/1/N_100.pdf.

Berman, N., Martin, P. & Mayer, T. (2012). How do different exporters react to exchange rate changes? *Quarterly Journal of Economics*, **127**(1), 437–92.

Bernard, A. B., Redding, S. & Schott, P. (2011). Multi-product firms and trade liberalization. *QuarterlyJournal of Economics*, **126**, 1271–318.

Berry, S. (1994). Estimating discrete-choice models of product differentiation. *RAND Journal of Economics*, **25**(2), 242–62.

Bils, M. & Klenow, P. J. (2001). Quantifying quality growth. *American Economic Review*, **91**(4), 1006–30.

Blind, K., Mangelsdorf, A. & Pohlisch, J. (2018). The effects of cooperation in accreditation on international trade: Empirical evidence on ISO 9000 certifications. *International Journal of Production Economics*, **198**, 50–9.

Bogliaccini, J. A. (2013). Trade liberalization: Deindustrialization, and inequality: Evidence from middle-income Latin American countries. *Latin American Research Review*, **48**(2), 79–105.

Brady, D., Kaya, Y. & Gereffi, G. (2011). Stagnating industrial employment in Latin America. *Work and Occupations*, **38**(2), 179–220.

Brambilla, I. & Porto, G. (2016). High-income export destinations, quality and wages. *Journal of International Economics*, **98**(C), 21–35.

Brambilla, I., Lederman, D. & Porto, G. (2012). Exports, export destinations, and skills. *American Economic Review*, **102**(7), 3406–38.

Brambilla, I., Lederman, D. & Porto, G. (2019). Exporting firms and the demand for skilled tasks. *Canadian Journal of Economics*, **52**(2). DOI: https://doi.org/10.1111/caje.12382.

Broda, C. & Romalis, J. (2011). Identifying the relationship between trade and exchange rate volatility. In T. Ito & A. K. Rose, eds., *Commodity Prices and Markets*, East Asia Seminar on Economics, Vol. 20. Chicago, IL: National Bureau of Economic Research, pp. 79–118.

Broda, C. & Weinstein, D. E. (2006). Globalization and the gains from variety. *Quarterly Journal of Economics*, **121**(2), 541–85.

Bruschi, V., Shershneva, K., Dolgopolova, I., Canavari, M. & Teuber, R. (2015). Consumer perception of organic food in emerging markets: Evidence from Saint Petersburg, Russia. *Agribusiness*, **31**(3), 414–32.

Chakraborty, B. S. & Sarkar, A. (2008). Trade, wage inequality and the vent for surplus. In S. Marjit & E. S. H. Yu, eds., *Contemporary and Emerging Issues in Trade Theory and Policy (Frontiers of Economics and Globalization, Vol. 4)*. Bingley: Emerald, pp. 251–73. https://doi.org/10.1016/S1574-8715(08)04013-X.

Chakraborty, B. S. & Sarkar, A. (2010). Trade and wage inequality with endogenous skill formation. In B. Basu, S. R. Chakravarty, B. K. Chakrabarti & K. Gangopadhyay, eds., *Econophysics and Economics of Games, Social Choices and Quantitative Techniques*. New Economic Windows. Milan: Springer, pp. 306–19. https://doi.org/10.1007/978-88-470-1501-2_30.

Chaudhuri, S. & Yabuuchi, S. (2008). Foreign capital and skilled-unskilled wage inequality in a developing economy with non-traded goods. In S. Marjit & E. Yu, eds., *Contemporary and Emerging Issues in Trade Theory and Policy*. Bingley: Emerald, pp. 225–50.

Chen, M. W., Lu, C. & Tian, Y. (2021). Export price and quality adjustment: The role of financial stress and exchange rate. *Economic Modelling*, **96**(2), 336–45.

Chen, N. & Juvenal, L. (2014). *Quality, Trade, and Exchange Rate Pass-Through*. IMF Working Paper 2014/042. Washington, DC: International Monetary Fund. www.imf.org/en/Publications/WP/Issues/2016/12/31/Quality-Trade-and-Exchange-Rate-Pass-Through-41416.

Chiang, S. C. & Masson, R. (1988). Domestic industrial structure and export upgrading: A quality signaling approach. *International Economic Review*, **29**, 261–70.

Clougherty, A. J. & Grajek, M. (2008). The impact of ISO 9000 diffusion on trade and FDI: A new institutional analysis. *Journal of International Business Studies*, **39**(4), 613–33.

Clougherty, A. J. & Grajek, M. (2014). International standards and international trade: Empirical evidence from ISO 9000 diffusion. *International Journal of Industrial Organization*, **36**, 70–82.

Commander, S., Kangasniemi, M. & Winters, L. A. (2004). The brain drain: Curse or boon? A survey of the literature. In R. E. Baldwin & L. A. Winters, eds., *Challenges to Globalization: Analyzing the Economics*. Chicago, IL: University of Chicago Press, pp. 235–78.

Das, S. K. & Bandyopadhyay, A. (2003). Quality signals and export performance: A micro-level study, 1989–97. *Economic and Political Weekly*, **38**(39), 4135–43.

Das, S. P. (2003). Trade and relative wage in a global economy. *Review of International Economics*, **11**(2), 397–411.

Davis, D. (1996). Trade liberalization and income distribution. NBER Working Paper 5693. Cambridge, MA: National Bureau of Economic Research. www.nber.org/system/files/working_papers/w5693/w5693.pdf.

Di Comite, F., Thisse, J. & Vandenbussche, H. (2014). Verti-zontal differentiation in export markets. *Journal of International Economics*, **93**(1), 50–66.

Didier, T. & Pinat, M. (2013). *How Does Trade Cause Growth?* West Lafayette, IN: Purdue University, Global Trade Analysis Project. www.gtap.agecon.purdue.edu/resources/download/6158.pdf.

Dongwen, T., Hu, N., Wang, X. & Huang, L. (2016). Trade margins, quality upgrading, and China's agri-food export growth. *China Agricultural Economic Review*, **8**(2), 277–98.

Donnenfeld, S. & Mayer, W. (1987). The quality of export products and optimal trade policy. *International Economic Review*, **28**(1), 159–74.

Dornbusch, R., Fischer, S. & Samuelson, P. A. (1977). Comparative advantage, trade, and payments in a Ricardian model with a continuum of goods. *American Economic Review*, **67**(5), 823–39.

Dunu, S. E. & Ayokanmbi, F. M. (2008). The impact of ISO 9000 certification on the financial performance of organizations. *Journal of Global Business Issues*, **2**(2), 135–44.

Ehrhart, H., Le Goff, M., Rocher, E. & Singh, R. J. (2014). *Does Migration Foster Exports? Evidence from Africa*. Policy Research Working Paper 6739. Washington, DC: World Bank. https://documents1.worldbank.org/curated/en/520651468194076878/pdf/WPS6739.pdf.

Elfenbein, D. W., Fisman, R. & McManus, B. (2015). Market structure, reputation, and the value of quality certification. *American Economic Journal: Microeconomics*, **7**(4), 83–108.

Fajgelbaum, P., Grossman, G. M. & Helpman, E. (2011). Income distribution, product quality, and international trade. *Journal of Political Economy*, **119**(4), 721–65.

Falvey, R. E. & Kierzkowski, H. (1987). Product quality, intra-industry trade and (im)perfect competition. In H. Kierzkowski, ed., *Protection and Competition in International Trade: Essays in Honor of W. M. Corden.* Oxford: Basil Blackwell, pp. 143–61.

Fan, H., Li, Y. A. & Yeaple, S. R. (2018). On the relationship between quality and productivity: Evidence from China's accession to the WTO. *Journal of International Economics*, **110**(C), 28–49.

Feenstra, R. (1994). New product varieties and the measurement of international prices. *American Economic Review*, **84**(1), 157–77.

Feenstra, R. C. & Hanson, G. H. (1996). Foreign investment, outsourcing and relative wages. In R. Feenstra, G. Grossman & D. Irwin, eds., *Political Economy of Trade Policies: Essays in Honor of J. N. Bhagwati.* Cambridge, MA: MIT Press, pp. 89–127.

Feenstra, R. & Romalis, J. (2014). International prices and endogenous quality. *Quarterly Journal of Economics*, **129**, 477–527.

Felbermayr, G. J. & Toubal, F. (2012). Revisiting the trade-migration nexus: Evidence from new OECD data. *World Development*, **40**(5), 928–37.

Ferro, E. (2011). *Signaling and Technological Marketing Tools for Exporters*. World Bank Policy Research Working Paper No. 5547. DOI: https://doi.org/10.1596/1813-9450-5547.

Fields, G. (1990). Labor market modeling and the urban informal sector: Theory and evidence. In D. Turnham, B. Salomé & A. Schwarz, eds., *The Informal Sector Revisited*. Paris: OECD, pp. 49–69.

Fieler, A. C., Eslava, M. & Xu, D. Y. (2018). Trade, quality upgrading, and input linkages: Theory and evidence from Colombia. *American Economic Review*, **108**(1), 109–46.

Fischer, C. (2010). Food quality and product export performance: An empirical investigation of the EU situation. *Journal of International Food & Agribusiness Marketing*, **22**(3–4), 210–33.

Flam, H. & Helpman, E. (1987). Vertical product differentiation and North–South trade. *American Economic Review*, **77**, 810–22.

Gabszewicz, J. & Thisse, J. (1979). Price competition, quality and income disparities. *Journal of Economic Theory*, **20**(3), 340–59.

Gabszewicz, J. & Wauthy, X. (2002). Quality underprovision by a monopolist when quality is not costly. *Economics Letters*, **77**(1), 65–72.

Ganguly, S. & Acharyya, R. (2020). Emigration, tax on remittances and export quality. *South Asian Journal of Macroeconomics and Public Finance*, **10**(1), 1–32. DOI: https://doi.org/10.1177/2277978720980236.

Ganguly, S. & Acharyya, R. (2021). Trade liberalization, export quality, and three dimensions of wage inequality. *Review of Development Economics*, **25**(4), 2157–79.

Ganguly, S. & Acharyya, R. (2022a). Asymmetric quality effect of input trade liberalization. In S. Bagli, G. Chakrabarti & P. Guha, eds., *Persistent and Emerging Challenges to Development: Insights for Policy-Making in India*. Singapore: Springer Nature, pp. 15–38.

Ganguly, S. & Acharyya, R. (2022b). Devaluation, export quality and employment in a small dependent economy. *Journal of Economic Development*, March, 47(1).

Genc, M., Gheasi, M., Nijkamp, P. & Poot, J. (2011). *The Impact of Immigration on International Trade: A Meta-analysis*. Discussion Paper No. 6145. Bonn: IZA. https://docs.iza.org/dp6145.pdf.

Gopinath, G. & Rigobon, R. (2008). Sticky borders. *Quarterly Journal of Economics,* **123**(2), 531–75.

Gruen, F. H. & Corden, M. W. (1970). A tariff that worsens the terms of trade. In I. A. McDougall & R. H. Snape, eds., *Studies in International Economics*. Amsterdam: North-Holland, pp. 55–8.

Hallak, J. C. (2006). Product quality and the direction of trade. *Journal of International Economics*, **68**(1), 238–65.

Hallak, J. C. & Schott, P. (2011). Estimating cross-country differences in product quality. *Quarterly Journal of Economics*, **126**(1), 417–74.

Hallak, J. C. & Sivadasan, J. (2013). Product and process productivity: Implications for quality choice and conditional exporter premia. *Journal of International Economics*, **91**(1), 53–67.

Hausmann, R. & Klinger, B. (2006). *Structural Transformation and Patterns of Comparative Advantage in the Product Space.* Center for International Development and KSG Faculty Research Working Paper Series CID-128 and RWP06-041. Cambridge, MA: Harvard Kennedy School. www.hks.harvard.edu/ publications/structural-transformation-and-patterns-comparative-advantage-product-space.

Hausmann, R., Hwang, J. & Rodrik, D.(2007). What you export matters. *Journal of Economic Growth*, **12**(1), 1–25.

Henn, C., Papageorgiou, C. & Spatafora, N. (2013). *Export Quality in Developing Countries.* IMF Working Paper 13/108. Washington, DC: International Monetary Fund. www.imf.org/external/pubs/ft/wp/2013/ wp13108.pdf.

Hidalgo, C. A., Klinger, B., Barabasi, A. L. & Hausmann, R. (2007). The product space conditions the development of nations. *Science*, **317**(5837), 482–7.

Hu, C., Parsely, D. & Tan, Y. (2017). *Exchange Rate Induced Quality Upgrading: A Firm Level Perspective.* MPRA Paper No. 80506. Munich: Munich Personal RePEc Archive. https://mpra.ub.uni-muenchen.de/id/ eprint/80506.

Hudson, J. & Jones, P. (2003). International trade in quality goods: Signalling problems for developing countries. *Journal of International Development*, **15**(8), 999–1013.

Hui, X., Saeedi, S. & Tadelis, S. (2019). Certification, reputation and entry: An empirical analysis. *Management Science*, **65**(12), 5449–60.

Hummels, D. & Klenow, P. (2005). The variety and quality of a nation's exports. *American Economic Review*, **95**(3), 704–23.

Jan-Benedict, E.M. S. (1989). Product quality: An investigation into the concept and how it is perceived by consumers. *International Journal of Research in Marketing*, **6**, 299–304.

Janssen, M. & Hamm, U. (2012). Product labelling in the market for organic food: Consumer preferences and willingness-to-pay for different organic certification logos. *Food Quality and Preference*, **25**(1), 9–22.

Jin, G. Z. & Leslie, P. (2003). The effect of information on product quality: Evidence from restaurant hygiene grade cards. *Quarterly Journal of Economics*, **118**(2), 409–51.

Jones, R. W. (1965). The structure of simple general equilibrium models. *Journal of Political Economy*, **73**, 557–72.

Jones, R. W. & Marjit, S. (1992). International trade and endogenous production structure. In W. Neufeind & R. Riezman, eds., *Economic Theory and International Trade: Essays in Memoriam J. Trout Rader*. Berlin: Springer-Verlag, pp. 173–96.

Khandelwal, A. (2010). The long and short (of) quality ladders. *Review of Economic Studies*, **77**, 1450–76.

Klein, B. & Leffler, K. B. (1981). The role of market forces in assuring contractual performance. *Journal of Political Economy*, **89**(4), 615–41.

Krugman, P. R. (1979). Increasing returns, monopolistic competition, and international trade. *Journal of International Economics*, **9**(4), 469–79.

Kugler, M. & Verhoogen, E. (2012). Prices, plant size, and product quality. *Review of Economic Studies*, **79**(1), 307–39.

Li, H., Ma, H. & Xu, Y. (2015). How do exchange rate movements affect Chinese exports? A firm-level investigation. *Journal of International Economics*, **97**(1), 148–61.

Linder, S. B. (1961). *An Essay on Trade and Transformation*. Stockholm: Almqvist & Wicksell.

Ma, Y. & Dei, F. (2009). Product quality, wage inequality, and trade liberalization. *Review of International Economics*, **17**(2), 244–60.

Manova, K. & Zhang, Z. (2012). *Multi-product Firms and Product Quality*. NBER Working Paper No. 18637. DOI: https://doi.org/10.3386/w18637.

Marcouiller, D. & Young, L. (1995). The black hole of graft: The predatory state and the informal economy. *American Economic Review*, **85**(3), 630–46.

Marjit, S. (2003). Economic reform and informal wage: A general equilibrium analysis. *Journal of Development Economics*, **72**, 371–8.

Marjit, S. & Acharyya, R. (2003). *International Trade, Wage Inequality and the Developing Countries: A General Equilibrium Approach*. Heidelberg: Physica/Springer-Verlag.

Marjit, S. & Acharyya, R. (2009). Trade and wages. In R. S. Rajan & K. Reinert, eds., *Princeton Encyclopedia of the World Economy*. Princeton, NJ: Princeton University Press, 1108–1112.

Marjit, S. & Beladi, H. (1999). Complementarity between import protection and import promotion. *Journal of Economic Theory*, **86**, 280–5.

Marjit, S. & Kar, S. (2005). Emigration and wage inequality. *Economics Letters*, **88**(1), 141–5.

Marjit, S. & Kar, S. (2011). *The Outsiders: Economic Reform and Informal Labour in a Developing Economy.* New Delhi: Oxford University Press.

Marjit, S., Ganguly, S. & Acharyya, R. (2020). Minimum wage, trade and unemployment in general equilibrium. *International Journal of Economic Theory*, 1–14. DOI: https://doi.org/10.1111/ijet.12264.

Marjit, S., Kar, S. & Beladi, H. (2007). Trade and informal wages. *Review of Developmemt Economics*, **11**(2), 313–20.

Martín, L. & Rodríguez, D. (2004). Pricing to market at firm level. *Review of World Economics (Weltwirtschaftliches Archiv)*, **140**(2), 302–20.

Maskus, K. E., Otsuki, T. & Wilson, J. S. (2005). *The Cost of Compliance with Product Standards for Firms in Developing Countries: An Econometric Study.* Policy Research Working Paper No. 3590. Washington, DC: World Bank. http://hdl.handle.net/10986/8961.

Matsuyama, K. (2000). A Ricardian model with a continuum of goods under nonhomothetic preferences: Demand complementarities, income distribution, and North–South trade. *Journal of Political Economy*, **108**(6), 1093–120.

McKenzie, M. D. (1999).The impact of exchange rate volatility on international trade flows. *Journal of Economic Surveys*, **13**(1), 71–106.

Melitz, M. J. & Ottaviano, G. I. P. (2008). Market size, trade, and productivity. *Review of Economic Studies,* **75**, 295–316.

Montiel, I., Husted, B. W. & Christmann, P. (2012). Using private management standard certification to reduce information asymmetries in corrupt environments. *Strategic Management Journal*, **33**(9), 1103–13.

Murphy, K. M. & Shleifer, A. (1997). Quality and trade. *Journal of Development Economics,* **53**, 1–15.

Mussa, M. & Rosen, S. (1978). Monopoly and product quality. *Journal of Economic Theory*, **18**, 301–17.

Nelson, P. (1974). Advertising as information. *Journal of Political Economy*, **82**(4), 729–54.

Ollinger, M. & Bovay, J. (2020). Producer response to public disclosure of food-safety information. *American Journal of Agricultural Economics*, **102**(1), 186–201.

Ortega, D. L., Wang, H. H., Wu, L. & Olynk, N. J. (2011). Modeling heterogeneity in consumer preferences for select food safety attributes in China. *Food Policy*, **36**(2), 318–24.

Peuckert, J. (204). What shapes the impact of environmental regulation on competitiveness? Evidence from executive opinion surveys. *Environmental Innovation and Societal Transitions,* **10**, 77–94.

Piveteau, P. & Smagghue, G. (2019). Estimating firm product quality using trade data. *Journal of International Economics*, **118**(C), 217–32.

Potoski, M. & Prakash, A. (2009). Information asymmetries as trade barriers: ISO 9000 increases international commerce. *Journal of Policy Analysis and Management,* **28**(2), 221–38.

Rashid, S. (1988). Quality in contestable markets: A historical problem? *Quarterly Journal of Economics*, **103**(1), 245–9.

Rauch, J. E. & Casella, A. (2003). Overcoming informational barriers to international resource allocation: Prices and ties. *Economic Journal,* **113** (484), 21–42.

Rauch, J. E. & Trindade, V. (2002). Ethnic Chinese network in international trade. *Review of Economics and Statistics*, **84**(1), 116–30.

Raychaudhuri, A., Acharyya, R., Marjit, S., Bhattacharyya, D., Rahman, M. & Tipu, M. A. (2003). *Trade Potentials of South Asian Economies under the New Global Trade Regime Regime:The Role of Some Non-price Factors (Case Study of India, Bangladesh and Sri Lanka)*. SANEI-III Project 2002-2003. Bangladesh: South Asia Network of Economic Research Institutionsin collaboration with the Centre for Policy Dialogue, Bangladesh and the Centre for Studies in Social Sciences, Calcutta.

Rodrik, D. (2006). What's so special about China's exports? *China &World Economy*, **14**(5), 1–19. http://gesd.free.fr/rodrik6.pdf.

Rogers, C. A. & Swinnerton, K. A. (2004). A Model of Informal Sector Labor Markets. Unpublished paper.

Sanetra, C. & Marban, R. M. (2007). The Answer to the Global Quality Challenge: A National Quality Infrastructure. Physikalisch-Technische Bundesanstalt, Organization of the American States and Sistema Interamericano de Metrología. www.ptb.de/cms/fileadmin/internet/fachabtei lungen/abteilung_9/9.3_internationale_zusammenarbeit/publikationen/ 102_National_QI/PTB_Q5_National_QI_EN.pdf.

Schott, P. K. (2004). Across-product versus within-product specialization in international trade. *Quarterly Journal of Economics*, **119**(2), 647–78.

Shaked, A. & Sutton, J. (1982). Relaxing price competition through product differentiation. *Review of Economic Studies*, **49**(1), 3–13.

Shapiro, C. (1983). Premiums for high quality products as returns to reputations. *Quarterly Journal of Economics*, **98**(4), 659–80.

Sung, J. K. & Reinert, K. A. (2009). Standards and institutional capacity: An examination of trade in food and agricultural products. *International Trade Journal*, **23**(1), 54–77.

Sutton, J. (2001). *Rich Trades, Scarce Capabilities: Industrial Development Revisited*. Economics of Industry Discussion Paper No. EI/28. London:

Suntory and Toyota International Centres for Economics and Related Disciplines. http://eprints.lse.ac.uk/2037/.

Swinnerton, K. A. (1996). Minimum wages in an equilibrium search model with diminishing returns to labor in production. *Journal of Labor Economics*, **14**(2), 340–55.

Thirkell, P. C. & Dau, R. (1998). Export performance: Success determinants for New Zealand manufacturing exporters. *European Journal of Marketing*, **32**(9–10), 813–29.

Thorbecke, W. & Smith, G. (2010). How would an appreciation of the renminbi and other East Asian currencies affect China's exports? *Review of International Economics*, **18**(1), 95–108.

Tirole, J. (1988). *The Theory of Industrial Organization*. Cambridge, MA: MIT Press.

Vandenbussche, H. (2014). *Quality in Exports*. European Economy – Economic Papers 528. Brussels: European Commission. http://ec.europa.eu/economy_finance/publications/.

Van Loo, E. J., Caputo, V., Nayga, Jr., R. M., Meullenet, J.-F. & Ricke, S. C. (2011). Consumers' willingness to pay for organic chicken breast: Evidence from choice experiment. *Food Quality and Preference*, **22**(7), 603–13.

Verhoogen, E. A. (2008). Trade, quality upgrading, and wage inequality in the Mexican manufacturing sector. *Quarterly Journal of Economics*, **123**(2), 489–530.

Wei, Y. & Balasubramanyam, V. N. (2006). Diaspora and development. *World Economy*, **29**(11), 1599–609.

Wei, Y., Liu, X., Lu, J. & Yang, J. (2017). Chinese migrants and their impact on homeland development. *World Economy*, **40**(11), 2354–77.

Xu, B. (2003). Trade liberalization, wage inequality and endogeneously determined non-traded goods. *Journal of International Economics*, **60**(2), 417–31.

Yu, Z. (2013). *Exchange Rate Pass-Through, Firm Heterogeneity and Product Quality: A Theoretical Analysis*. Globalization and Monetary Policy Institute Working Paper No. 141. Dallas, TX: Federal Reserve Bank of Dallas. www.dallasfed.org/assets/documents/institute/wpapers/2013/0141.pdf.

Zapechelnyuk, A. (2020). Optimal quality certification. *American Economic Review: Insights*, **2**(2), 161–76.

Zhu, S. & Trefler, D. (2005). Trade and inequality in developing countries: A general equilibrium analysis. *Journal of International Economics*, **65**(1), 21–48.

Acknowledgements

Insights into the general equilibrium structures that lay the foundation of this book have been greatly shaped and influenced by several teachers, co-authors and, of course, students. Among them, special mention must be made of Ronald W. Jones, Sugata Marjit and (late) Kalyan K. Sanyal. We also thank Ajitava Ray Chaudhuri, Jayanta Dwibedi, Wilfred Ethier, Triptendu Ghosh, Kausik Gupta, Saibal Kar, Ravi Kumar, Kamal Saggi, Rahul Sen and Thierry Verdier, for helpful discussions and comments on many of the issues discussed here; and Kenneth A. Reinert, editor of this series, and two anonymous reviewers for their valued comments and suggestions on an earlier draft of the Element.

Shrimoyee Ganguly thanks her parents, Sandhya Ganguly and Sanjay Gangopadhyay, for their unconditional mental support throughout her educational journey and in every other walk of life.

Cambridge Elements ☰

International Economics

Kenneth A. Reinert
George Mason University

Kenneth A. Reinert is Professor of Public Policy in the Schar School of Policy and Government at George Mason University where he directs the Global Commerce and Policy master's degree program. He is author of *An Introduction to International Economics: New Perspectives on the World Economy* with Cambridge University Press and coauthor of *Globalization for Development: Meeting New Challenges* with Oxford University Press. He is also editor of *The Handbook of Globalisation and Development* with Edward Elgar and co-editor of the two-volume *Princeton Encyclopedia of the World Economy* with Princeton University Press.

About the Series

International economics is a distinct field with both fundamental theoretical insights and increasing empirical and policy relevance. The *Cambridge Elements in International Economics* showcases this field, covering the subfields of international trade, international money and finance, and international production, and featuring both established researchers and new contributors from all parts of the world. It aims for a level of theoretical discourse slightly above that of the *Journal of Economic Perspectives* to maintain accessibility. It extends Cambridge University Press' established reputation in international economics into the new, digital format of *Cambridge Elements*. It attempts to fill the niche once occupied by the *Princeton Essays in International Finance*, a series that no longer exists.

There is a great deal of important work that takes place in international economics that is set out in highly theoretical and mathematical terms. This new Elements does not eschew this work but seeks a broader audience that includes academic economists and researchers, including those working in international organisations, such as the World Bank, the International Monetary Fund, and the Organisation for Economic Co-operation and Development.

Cambridge Elements ≡

International Economics

Elements in the Series

Printed in the United States
by Baker & Taylor Publisher Services